An illustrated
country year

*nature uncovered
month by month*

Celia Lewis

BLOOMSBURY

LONDON · NEW DELHI · NEW YORK · SYDNEY

First published in 2013

Bloomsbury Publishing Plc, 50 Bedford Square, London WC1B 3DP
Bloomsbury USA, 175 Fifth Avenue, New York, NY 10010

www.bloomsbury.com
www.bloomsburyusa.com

Bloomsbury Publishing, London, New Delhi, New York and Sydney

A CIP catalogue record for this book is available from the British Library
Library of Congress Cataloging-in-Publication Data has been applied for

Commissioning Editor: Julie Bailey
Project Editor: Julie Bailey
Design by Julie Dando, Fluke Art

ISBN (print) 978-1-4081-8134-8
ISBN (ebook) 978-1-4081-8688-6

Printed in China

10 9 8 7 6 5 4 3 2 1

MIX
Paper from
responsible sources
FSC® C101537

Contents

For

Joshy, Raffy, Lani, Algie, Willa and Orlando

If you don't open the door
You'll never know what's on the other side

I believe in God only I spell it 'Nature'
Frank Lloyd Wright

Having lived all my life in the country I realise more and more how lucky we are in the northern hemisphere to live in a temperate part of the world with four distinct seasons. Our climate may be changing but nature has a wonderful way of putting things right – a long cold winter and you'd expect everything to be behind for the year, but somehow it always catches up and the same things flower or fly at the same time each month year on year.

Noticing what is happening around us in the natural world makes a walk in the country so much more interesting and enjoyable – spotting the first bluebell or finding a jewel-like Jay's feather, or even figuring out who's eaten a nut or fir cone. Learning who or what is about using all sorts of signs is an important and fundamental part of country life.

The following pages are set out in months, each containing just a few of the flowers, birds or other wildlife you might see at that particular time of year, and some ideas and suggestions for things to make or eat from foraged fruit or objects.

Inevitably in some years events will happen at a different time and seasons arrive earlier in the south than the north of the UK. But each month offers a glimpse of what is out there, to delight and perhaps inspire you with the desire to learn more of nature's rich tapestry.

January

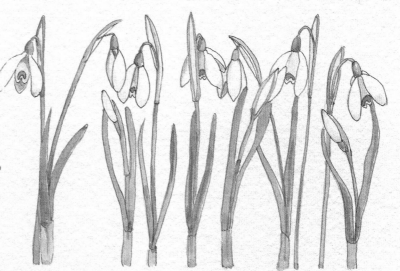

Of grass do grow in Janiveer,
It grows the worse for all the year

Grass and all other growing plants are geared up to rest during the winter so an unusual warm spell this month is actually a bad thing if it lasts long enough to fool them into thinking it's spring. Of course there are some plants that do start their growth during this cold dark period, bulbs being one, and the snowdrop is the first to bravely put forth its flowers.

Frosts are frequent at this time of year and there may even be snow with a prolonged cold period. Anything that has begun to grow, and in some cases growth is triggered by the lengthening days rather than temperature, will simply stop and pick up again when the coldest spell has passed.

Animals that hibernate will still be tucked up in their sheltered accommodation. The dormouse (not for nothing is it named 'dor' from the Latin 'dormire' meaning to sleep) remains dormant from October to May. It achieves this feat by slowing its body metabolism down by 90%. Dormice can live for up to 5 years and are recognisable by their golden colour and thick furry tail that they wrap around themselves when sleeping. They are nocturnal and spend most of their waking hours hunting for their food of flowers, berries and nuts, staying above ground as much as possible. See September (page 144) for how to recognise a hazel nut that has been eaten by a dormouse.

January

Is it a coot or a moorhen?

The **Coot** (*Fulica atra*) is the only all-black water bird with a very conspicuous white frontal shield and bill. It is a rather quarrelsome bird and can often be seen chasing others. Its call is less musical than the Moorhen and sounds like 'kwok' or 'ke-kewk' – it might be imagined to be calling 'coot'. Coots take a very long run across the water to take off and have a heavy laboured flight.

Coot

Moorhen

The **Moorhen** (*Gallinula chloropus*) is also mainly black but with a white line of feathers along the flank and conspicuous white under-tail coverts that are flicked up and down. Young birds have a more olive hue. The bill is a distinct red with yellow tip and the green legs have a reddish garter at the top. Moorhens are also rather clumsy fliers with laboured take-offs. Their call of 'prrrrrrk', which they make even at night, will be well known to anyone who lives near water.

Mosses

Large White-moss
(*Leucobryum glaucum*)

There are literally hundreds of different types of moss – the only thing they have in common is that they are green and prefer damp places. One of the loveliest is Large White-moss (*Leucobryum glaucum*) (known in my family as 'moss pets' because it's impossible to resist holding a bit in your hand and stroking it!), which grows in small lumps, most commonly in pine woods. If turned over by a bird this moss has the ability to grow whichever way up it is and you can sometimes find completely green balls of it, apparently unattached to the earth. Many mosses can only be distinguished with the aid of a microscope but here are a few of the most common.

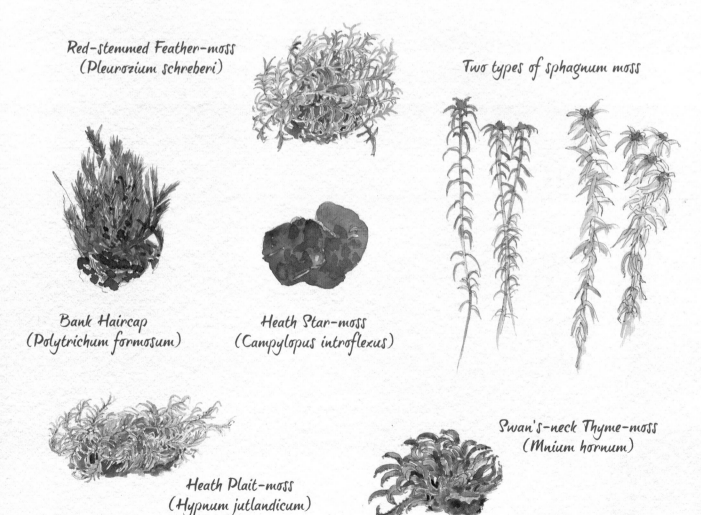

Red-stemmed Feather-moss
(*Pleurozium schreberi*)

Two types of sphagnum moss

Bank Haircap
(*Polytrichum formosum*)

Heath Star-moss
(*Campylopus introflexus*)

Swan's-neck Thyme-moss
(*Mnium hornum*)

Heath Plait-moss
(*Hypnum jutlandicum*)

Lichens

Lichens come in three types – crustose (encrusting), foliose (leafy) and fructicose (shrubby) – and can survive in conditions of heat or cold where no other plant can. They are sensitive to atmospheric pollution so are a good indicator of clean air – they are rarely found near industrial sites. A valuable resource for dyes, lichens also have antibiotic properties and were even used to pack ancient Egyptian mummies. Two very common lichen examples are Oakmoss (*Evernia prunastri*), an important ingredient in perfumes as it helps scent last longer, and Beard Lichen or Tree Moss (*Usnea barbata*), which is edible (but not nice) and contains lots of vitamin C.

Lecanora muralis: Found naturally on nutrient-rich and calcareous rocks and also found particularly on concrete, especially urban areas enriched with nitrogen such as from bird droppings. It usually forms a loose rosette and is often mistaken for chewing gum on paving stones.

Parmelia saxatilis: Widespread and locally common, found on rocks and acid-barked trees. Used for making yellow and brown dyes. According to superstition, it was believed to be an effective treatment for epilepsy if found growing on an old skull, especially that of an executed criminal.

Xanthoria parietina: Thrives in areas with nitrogen pollutants. Common in cities and near roads. Its name is from the Greek 'xanthos' meaning yellow. The Inuit of Greenland call it 'sunain anak', meaning the sun's excrement. Xanthoria is also used for yellow dye.

Diploicia canescens: Common in the south but rarer and mainly coastal in the north, especially areas with frequent fogs. A crustose lichen that forms rosettes, which is mostly found on rocks, walls and bark; prefers shade.

How to make a miniature moss tree

Here's an idea for a really unusual table decoration. Once you've made your tree you can add temporary adornments to it to suit your needs – perhaps a few red berries at Christmas, some sprigs of heather or other flowers to suit your colour scheme for a wedding or even some tiny foil-covered eggs at Easter.

YOU WILL NEED:

Lots of different mosses and lichen collected from various locations – lichen can be found on fallen branches

Florist's wire

Dry oasis ball approx. 8 cm diameter

Honeysuckle, birch or other suitable stick for trunk, about 20 cm long

Small flowerpot

Florist's clay, stones, plasticine or cement

Push your stick (honeysuckle is lovely as it is twisted, and birch is pretty, but any stick will do) firmly into the oasis ball. Fill your flowerpot with the clay, stones or plasticine and push the stick down into it, making sure it is firm. Tuck some moss around the trunk to fill the pot.

Starting at the bottom, take small bunches of moss and wind a length of wire round, leaving a 4 cm tail sticking down. Push this into the dry oasis. Continue using different sorts of moss or lichen until your ball is covered – you will need more than you think. It doesn't matter if the moss is still damp, but when it has dried out it is a good idea to give it a couple of coats of spray varnish to stop little bits falling off. Eventually your tree will lose its colour, but the more kinds of moss you use the more varied the tree will remain.

Common Eider

Male Eider duck

The Common Eider (*Somateria mollissima*) is a diving sea duck found close to the coast. It is the UK's heaviest and also fastest flying duck. Eiders feed on shellfish, in particular mussels which they eat whole, crushing the shells in their gizzard. The duck lines her nest with eider down plucked from her own breast – eider down was once prized for filling pillows and duvets.

A famous colony of these ducks still live on the Farne Islands off the Northumberland coast. They became the first birds to have a protection order placed on them when St Cuthbert established one in the year 679. Northumberland still retains the Eider Duck as its county emblem.

The Moon

- It takes 29½ days for the moon to complete its orbit of Earth.

- The moon is an average of 384,403 km from the Earth. This figure is an average as the orbit is not a perfect circle.

- The moon is the only natural satellite of the Earth and the fifth largest in the solar system.

- The moon has no atmosphere, which means that there is no wind.

- The diameter of the moon is 3,476 km – one-quarter that of the Earth.

- The moon's gravitational pull has a major influence on our tides.

- The moon rotates at 10 mph compared to the Earth's 1,000 mph.

- From the Earth we only ever see one side of the moon – the other side is always hidden.

- Each month's full moon has a name: January – old moon; February – wolf moon; March – Lenten moon; April – egg moon; May – milk moon; June – flower moon; July – hay moon; August – grain moon; September – corn moon; October – harvest moon; November – hunter's moon; December – oak moon.

- A blue moon is the name given to a month that contains two full moons.

- The moon is the only extraterrestrial body that has been visited by man.

- The moon is not made of cheese!

waxing crescent   first quarter   waxing gibbous   full moon   waning gibbous   last quarter   waning crescent

January

Goldfinch

The Goldfinch (*Carduelis carduelis*) is one of the easiest birds to identify thanks to its distinct red, white and black face and black and gold wings. This beautiful bird feeds mainly on seeds and in particular thistles, including the teasel, as illustrated here. The female builds the nest, which is often on twigs towards the end of a branch and is a neat cup made of moss, grass and lichen and lined with feathers. She lays four to six pale blue eggs, finely spotted or streaked with purple, which hatch after 12–14 days. Only the female incubates the eggs while the male feeds her, but they both share the duties of feeding the young.

Chaffinch

The Chaffinch (*Fringilla coelebs*) is one of our most common birds and certainly the commonest finch found in the UK. The male's pinky-orange breast and cheeks, blue-grey cap and white wing patches make this an easy bird to recognise although the female is less colourful. Chaffinches feed on seeds and insects and can be seen foraging on the ground. Their nests are neat and round, made from moss and grass and bound with spider's webs.

Flint or flintstone

- Flint is a sedimentary rock, a variety of chert, found in chalk or limestone.

- Used during the Stone Age for blades as it splinters easily into shards when struck with another hard stone – known as knapping.

- Struck against steel it produces a spark to ignite tinder – before the age of steel this was done with iron pyrites.

- Part of a flintlock mechanism on a firearm to produce a spark to ignite the priming powder which in turn ignited the charge.

Chalk

- Type of limestone, a porous sedimentary rock composed of the mineral calcite.

- Formed on the sea bed 90 million years ago and thrown up in the movement of the earth to form cliffs and rolling downs.

- Holds water and releases it slowly in dry seasons.

- Used to make quicklime, lime mortar and to raise the pH level of acid soil.

- Used for blackboard chalk and gesso primer for artists.

- Used by sportsmen on hands to remove sweat and stop slipping.

- Used in toothpaste as a mild abrasive, in putty to pad out the linseed oil and as fingerprint powder.

Moules marinières

Mussels are a common crustacean found all around the coast and free for anyone to pick. Simply pull them off the rocks. Allow 500 ml (1 pint) per person. Wash the mussels and remove the beard (the coarse hairy bit that attached the shell to the rock) and any barnacles and discard shells that do not close when tapped. This is a very simple dish, most of the effort being in the preparation.

Serves 4

YOU WILL NEED:

2 litres (4 pints) mussels, cleaned

50 g unsalted butter

2 cloves of garlic, crushed (or to taste)

4 shallots, finely chopped

250 ml dry white wine

chopped parsley

Melt some butter in a large saucepan and fry the garlic and shallots for a few minutes. Add the white wine and bring to a fast boil.

Tip in the mussels and replace the lid.

Give the pan a good shake every now and then and cook until the mussels have opened – just a few minutes.

Serve in bowls with a large container in the centre of the table to throw the empty shells into. An empty shell makes a very handy pair of pincers to eat the mussels with.

To turn this into something really special add a bulb of very finely sliced fennel with the shallots and garlic and finish by stirring in some single cream.

Scots Pine

TYPE *Pinus sylvestris* is a widespread, evergreen coniferous tree with a straight scaly trunk and a rounded or flat-topped crown.

SIZE Up to 35 m high with 1 m trunk when mature.

BARK Thick and flaky. Dark brownish-grey at base of trunk and orange-pink on the upper parts. Scales drop off over the year. Sticky resin is exuded and creates a natural preservative for the wood.

FOLIAGE Needles in pairs, bluey-green.

CONES Seed cones are red at pollination, then turn pale brown, not becoming full size until their second year, when they turn green before reaching brown at maturity. Pollen cones or male flowers are yellow with reddish parts, releasing their pollen in mid to late spring.

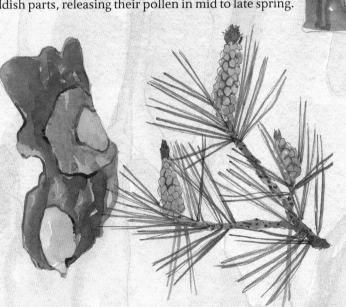

USES Paper pulp and sawn timber known as redwood or red deal, used among other things as roof timbers, furniture, telegraph poles and firewood, although care must be taken as it has a propensity to spit violently. It was also used in shipbuilding and the resin from the bark was once a source of tar and turpentine.

January

February

If Candlemas Day be fair and bright,

Winter will have another flight.

If Candlemas Day be cloud and rain,

Then winter will not come again.

Candlemas falls on 2 February and there is a country saying that goes: 'A farmer should on Candlemas Day, have half his corn and half his hay', which meant that although spring seems near in fact winter is only halfway through. But even in early February there are signs that growth is restarting and one of the first is Pussy Willow.

It is the catkin of the Goat Willow or Sallow (*Salix caprea*) that is also known as Pussy Willow, probably because it is covered in a fine grey fur like a kitten's paw. One of the first signs of spring, girls used to wear a sprig of Pussy Willow on Palm Sunday – it was said if they didn't they would get their hair pulled.

Even at this early time of the year some birds will already be thinking of nesting. Magpies are one of the first, as these clever birds rely on the nestlings and eggs of other birds to feed their own young. Rooks can be seen squabbling over suitable sites and stealing sticks from each other even though it will be more than a month before they get down to serious business.

Pussy Willow

February

Spring blossom

Blackthorn or sloe comes out in a froth of white blossom that looks spectacular against the black of the twigs and branches. The blossom is often a week or two later than that of the wild plum, which is generally the first blossom to show. A cold snap at this time of year often coincides with the flowering and is known as a 'blackthorn winter'. Wild cherry also flowers in March, the cherries, which are mainly stone, providing a popular food for birds.

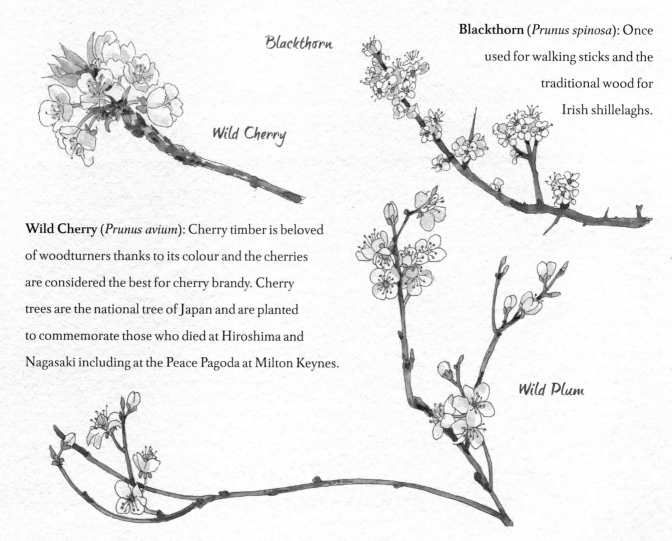

Blackthorn

Wild Cherry

Blackthorn (*Prunus spinosa*): Once used for walking sticks and the traditional wood for Irish shillelaghs.

Wild Cherry (*Prunus avium*): Cherry timber is beloved of woodturners thanks to its colour and the cherries are considered the best for cherry brandy. Cherry trees are the national tree of Japan and are planted to commemorate those who died at Hiroshima and Nagasaki including at the Peace Pagoda at Milton Keynes.

Wild Plum

Wild Plum or **Bulace** (*Prunus domestica*): Closely related to the French Mirabelle prune and comes in a variety of colours from red to yellow to green. All are very sour but make good jams and jellies.

Commonly found bones

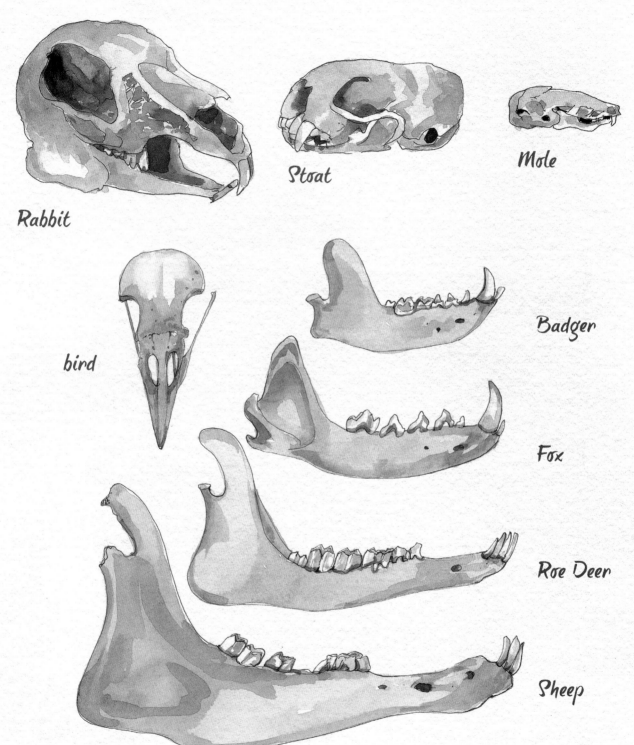

Rabbit

Stoat

Mole

bird

Badger

Fox

Roe Deer

Sheep

February

What type of crow is it?

The corvid family includes ravens, crows and jackdaws, as well as jays, magpies and choughs. Choughs have distinctively red bills and legs and inhabit coasts, but it's the crows that can be hard to tell apart.

Raven

Jackdaw

Carrion Crow

The **Raven** (*Corvus corax*) is the largest of the crow family – an all-black bird with glossy plumage that is found mainly in mountainous or hilly country but also favours sea cliffs and can be found in the grounds of the Tower of London.

The **Carrion Crow** (*Corvus corone*) is considerably smaller than the Raven with a small bill and, although similar in size to the Rook, it has an altogether smarter appearance and a greenish gloss to its coat. In North-west Scotland and Ireland the crows are two-toned pale grey and black and are known as **Hooded Crows** (*Corvus cornix*). Carrion and Hooded Crows were thought to be the same species until very recently, but are now considered separate species. Both can be found in a variety of habitats, but they overlap in very few places.

Rooks (*Corvus frugilegus*) are similar in size to crows, but their plumage has a more purplish gloss and they have a bare front to their face and a baggy-trouser look to their thighs. Rooks nest in colonies called rookeries and it's been said that if you see a flock of crows then they are Rooks (although crows do occasionally form flocks so this is not a fool-proof method of corvid identification).

Rook

The **Jackdaw** (*Corvus monedula*) is the smallest of the corvids, and can be recognised by its grey nape. Jackdaws nest in holes in trees or sometimes take over nests of the larger corvids, collecting twigs, hair and all sorts of other material to line it.

Jackdaw

Jay

Almost as small as the Jackdaw, the **Jay** (*Garrulus glandarius*) is the lone colourful member of the crow family in the UK, with its pinky-chestnut breast and beautiful blue-striped wing coverts. Listening for their screeching call is often the best way to confirm if any are around. Jays love acorns and bury them in the autumn as a store for later in the winter; their Latin name is derived from 'glandis' meaning acorn. As well as acorns, they eat nuts, seeds and insects and are also fond of nestlings in the spring.

February

Siskin

The Siskin (*Carduelis spinus*) is a pretty little bird, mainly a winter visitor to the UK, arriving in flocks from the continent. If you hear a mighty twittering coming from a tree but find it hard to spot a bird it is probably a group of Siskins on their way north or south. They particularly favour overwintering in alder and birch woods, feeding mainly on tree seeds such as those from alder cones.

How to make an oak apple necklace

Oak apples are made by gall wasps to give their larvae a safe place to grow. Look for them on the ground under oak trees or you may spot one still on the twig or leaf in winter. Although they are green and soft in the summer, by winter they will become hard and brown with a convenient hole where the gall wasp has left.

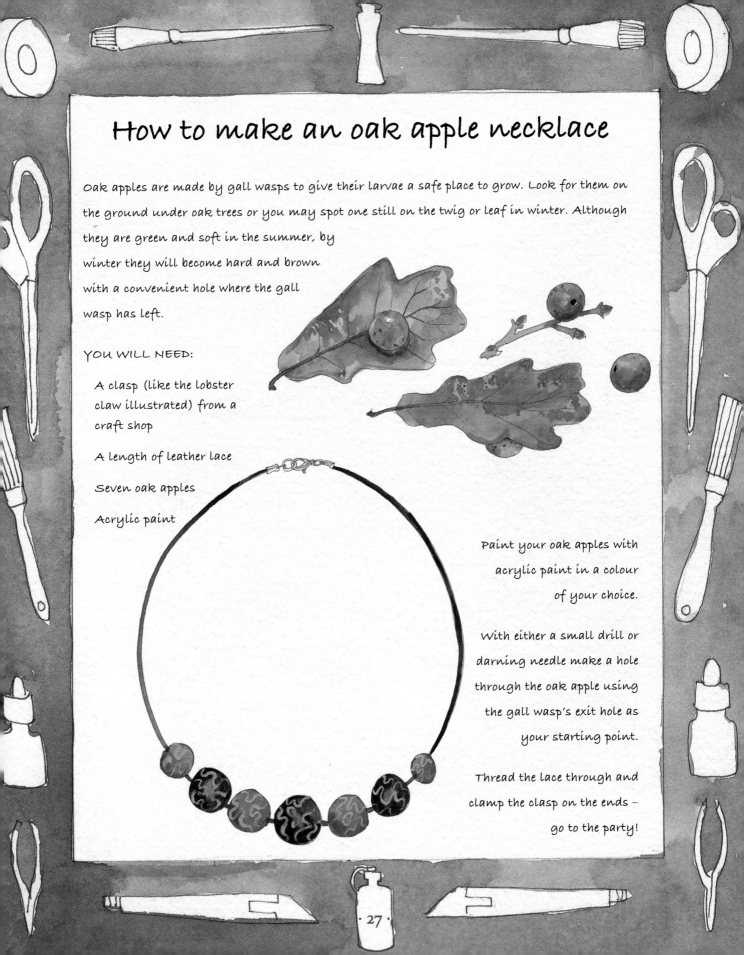

YOU WILL NEED:

A clasp (like the lobster claw illustrated) from a craft shop

A length of leather lace

Seven oak apples

Acrylic paint

Paint your oak apples with acrylic paint in a colour of your choice.

With either a small drill or darning needle make a hole through the oak apple using the gall wasp's exit hole as your starting point.

Thread the lace through and clamp the clasp on the ends – go to the party!

Deer

Deer differ from antelope in that they shed their antlers once a year, whereas an antelope retains them for life. The UK has five breeds of deer and no antelope although the Ibex and Chamois of Europe are types of antelope goats. Deer are browsers, eating whatever they come across, be it brambles, leaves, grass, crops or garden flowers. In some places deer are considered a nuisance and are culled.

Roe Deer hind

A deer's antlers fall off after the rut (breeding season) and almost immediately start to grow again. They grow at a prodigious rate (2.5 cm a day) and are covered in a kind of skin known as velvet, which provides oxygen and nutrients to the growing cartilage. When the antler finishes growing the velvet is rubbed off in strips and strings – at this stage the deer is known as being 'in tatters'. Once the velvet has gone the cartilage hardens into bone.

Roe Deer

Roe Deer (*Capreolus capreolus*) have been present in the UK since before the Mesolithic period of 6000–10,000 BC. They had been hunted to extinction by 1800 but were reintroduced by the Victorians and are now extremely common. Mating takes place in August but the fertilised egg does not implant until January – a process known as 'delayed implantation', which prevents them giving birth during the winter. One, two or even three fawns are born in May. Antlers are shed during November and December and the velvet of the new antlers will be clear by March.

Roe Deer fawn

Standing 60–70 cm at the shoulder and weighing 10–20 kg this is the smallest of our native deer. Roe give a short sharp bark rather like a dog when alarmed.

Fallow Deer

Thought to have been introduced by the Normans, Fallow Deer (*Dama dama*) come in a variety of colours, from almost completely white to completely black, but the most common colour is chestnut with white mottles. Similar in size to Sika Deer, the stags are easy to distinguish thanks to their magnificent broad antlers. The rut takes place in September to October and a single fawn is born in May or June.

Fallow Deer buck

Fallow Deer doe

Muntjac Deer

Muntjac Deer

These little deer *Muntiacus reevesi* are natives of South China and were introduced to the UK via Woburn Abbey, from where they escaped in the late 19th century. They are sometimes known as barking deer but more correctly as Reeves' Muntjac, after John Reeves who was an inspector with the East India Tea Company in 1812.

Standing 45–52 cm at the shoulder they weigh between 12 and 15 kg. Muntjac have no closed season for hunting as they can give birth at any time of year. The female is usually pregnant again within a few days of giving birth and weans her young at two months.

Red Deer

Weighing up to 190kg the Red Deer (*Cervus elaphus*) is the UK's largest mammal, although those living in hill country are slightly smaller than those living in parks. These deer can live up to 18 years and achieve 16 points on their antlers. Now confined in the wild to the Scottish Highlands and south-west England they were once found all over the country, protected in parks specifically for hunting.

The stags roar and grunt during the rut, which takes place between September and November when stags fight to mate with hinds, sometimes to the death and often causing injuries. The stags are at least 5 years old before they are capable of mating.

Red Deer shed their antlers between March and May and these are gnawed by the hinds as a welcome source of calcium.

Red Deer stag

Red Deer hind

Sika Deer

Between the Roe Deer and Red Deer in size, the pretty Sika Deer (*Cervus Nippon*) is similar to the Fallow Deer, with a mottled coat, but their antlers are more like those of the Red Deer, with a maximum of eight points. They were introduced from the Far East in 1860 and there are several subspecies living in parks but it is only the Japanese Sika that has been successful in living wild in the UK. Sika give birth to a single fawn in May.

Sika Deer stag

Great Crested Grebe

The Great Crested Grebe (*Podiceps cristatus*) is the largest of the grebe family and is found all over Europe. They are diving birds that feed on fish, small crustaceans, insects and frogs. They are renowned for their elaborate mating display, which is somewhat like synchronised swimming, with both birds diving and reappearing together with weed in their beaks. The birds then rear up by paddling madly, and offer the gift to each other chest to chest. Many other moves ensue until finally the two birds form a lasting bond.

Great Crested Grebes usually lay two white eggs and although the young stripy chicks are able to swim at hatching they tend to ride about on the backs of their parents. The adults dive, leaving the chick floating on the surface, who then has to swim after the parent when they re-emerge.

Once nearly hunted to extinction by the Victorians, who valued their elegant feathers, Great Crested Grebes have now made a comeback and can be commonly seen on rivers, lakes and reservoirs.

February

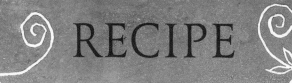

Nettle soup

This is a really nutritious, bright green and delicious soup. This is the time of year to make nettle soup – when the nettles are just coming up and tender. Later in the year they will have woody, stringy stems but will still be edible – the soup will simply need sieving. If any is available you can exchange the garlic for wild garlic or ransomes, for a truly foraged meal. Wear rubber or gardening gloves to pick your nettles and just pluck off the tops, or snip them into a bag with scissors – you'll need more than you think, about 50, as they will cook down considerably.

Serves 6 to 8

YOU WILL NEED:

125 g butter

500 g potatoes

1 large onion

2 garlic cloves

750 ml chicken or vegetable stock

50 nettle tops

salt, pepper and nutmeg

sour cream, to finishh

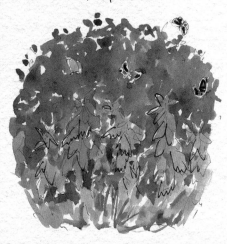

Peel and chop the potatoes, garlic and onions.

In a large pan melt the butter and fry the potatoes, garlic and onions until lightly browned.

Pour in the stock, stirring as you go, bring to the boil and add the nettle tops.

Simmer until the potato is soft – about 20 minutes.

Whizz in a liquidiser and season to taste.

To serve stir in a whirl of sour cream and twist over some black pepper – serve with warm crusty bread

Larch

TYPE *Larix decidua* is a fast-growing but fairly short-lived conifer growing to approximately 30 m, which turns yellow in winter and loses its needles. It is the only deciduous coniferous tree native to Europe.

BARK Pinky-brown with deep vertical crevices.

FOLIAGE Soft, thin, bright green needles 2–3 cm long that emerge in March.

CONES AND FLOWERS Male and larger female flowers on twigs. Forming cones turn reddish purple, ripening to light brown.

USES Prized for boat building thanks to its waterproof and durable qualities. Used for fencing as it is resistant to rot. The caber used for tossing at Scottish Highland Games is traditionally a larch.

February

March

*March comes in like a lion
and goes out like a lamb.*

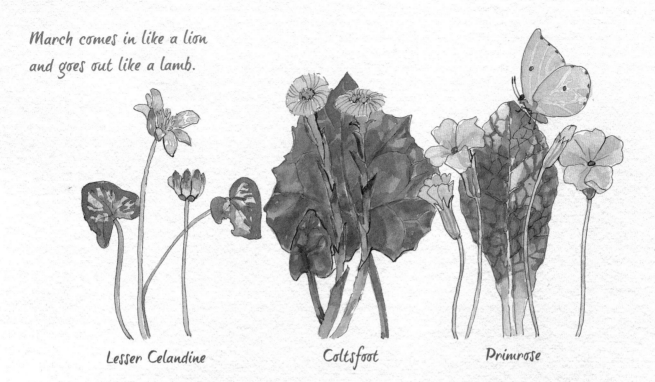

Lesser Celandine   Coltsfoot   Primrose

March is the first month in the Roman calendar, named after Mars, God of War. As the saying goes, it very often starts off windy but by the end, when spring is in sight, the weather should become more gentle and start to warm up. At last some signs of growth – in the south of England the third week in March is traditionally when the grass starts growing, a relief for anyone who owns stock.

A true harbinger of spring, the Chiffchaff (*Phylloscopus collybita*) arrives this month to breed and stays until September or October. It is easy bird to hear (though difficult to see) as it clearly says 'chiff chaff chiff chaff'. A summer visitor to northern Europe, this little bird is just 10 cm long, weighing no more than 9 g, yet it performs the amazing feat of flying all the way from its wintering grounds in West Africa, flying through the night and crossing the Sahara and Mediterranean, perhaps barely stopping for a rest.

One of the first flowers to herald spring is the aptly named Primrose (*Primula vulgaris*) whose name means 'first rose'. It is found all over the country but favours hedgerows and woods. Another spring plant, the Coltsfoot, is strange in that its flowers come up and bloom before the large hoof-shaped leaves appear. Its name comes from 'tussis ago', meaning to drive away a cough, and dried Coltsfoot flowers and leaves can be made into a tea to clear congestion and give relief from coughs. Lesser Celandine (*Ranunculus ficaria*) is sometimes called a 'spring messenger' as it too flowers from March. It is also known as Pilewort as the knobbly tubers resemble haemorrhoids and were therefore considered a cure for piles. The leaves were once also a valuable source of vitamin C to prevent scurvy.

March

Woodpeckers

Great Spotted Woodpecker

Woodpeckers may have been drumming on fine days since January but during March they're at their peak, establishing their territories and looking for a mate. The Great Spotted Woodpecker (*Dendrocopos major*) drums for 1 second, during which time it fits in eight to ten blows to its chosen sound board – usually a dead tree. The Lesser Spotted, or Barred, Woodpecker (*Dendrocopus minor*), although smaller, can be told apart as it manages up to 30 blows at a time. Fortunately woodpeckers have thicker skulls than other birds, which cushion the brain during drumming. A sharp 'chink' is uttered if the bird is alarmed.

Great Spotted Woodpeckers are black and white with a red patch under their tail-coverts, and the male also has a red nape and the juvenile a red crown. In the Lesser Spotted only the male and juvenile have red crowns and these birds are almost half the size of their larger cousins.

Woodpeckers all have a distinct undulating flight pattern, with the wings folded against the body during the dips.

Green Woodpecker

Larger than either of the two spotted woodpeckers, the Green Woodpecker (*Picus viridis*) or 'yaffle' spends a lot of time feeding on the ground looking for ants, its favourite food. If it finds an ant's nest it uses its tongue, which has barbs on the end of it, to extract them. The tongue is so long, up to 10 cm, that it has to be curled round the bird's skull. Green Woodpeckers do drum but not as loudly or frequently as the spotted woodpeckers and they also nest in holes in trees. All woodpeckers have extra-strong tails that they use to support their bodies when climbing trees.

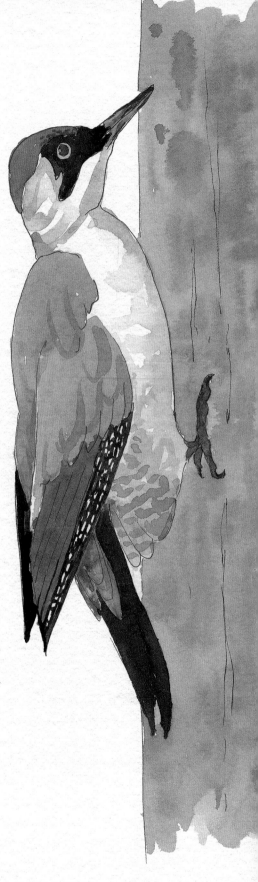

Scarlet Elf Cup

This eye-catching fungus *Sarcoscypha coccinea* with its brilliant scarlet cups is a saprophyte that grows on decaying vegetation, particularly fallen branches on the damp forest floor. It appears in late winter to early spring.

How to make a birch bark mirror

You can always fit another mirror in somewhere around the house and no one will have seen one quite like this.

YOU WILL NEED:

  Piece of MDF (50 cm square)

  Mirror (30 cm square)

  Birch bark

  Craft or Stanley knife

  Honeysuckle to finish

  Glue

  Sandpaper

  Varnish

  Panel pins

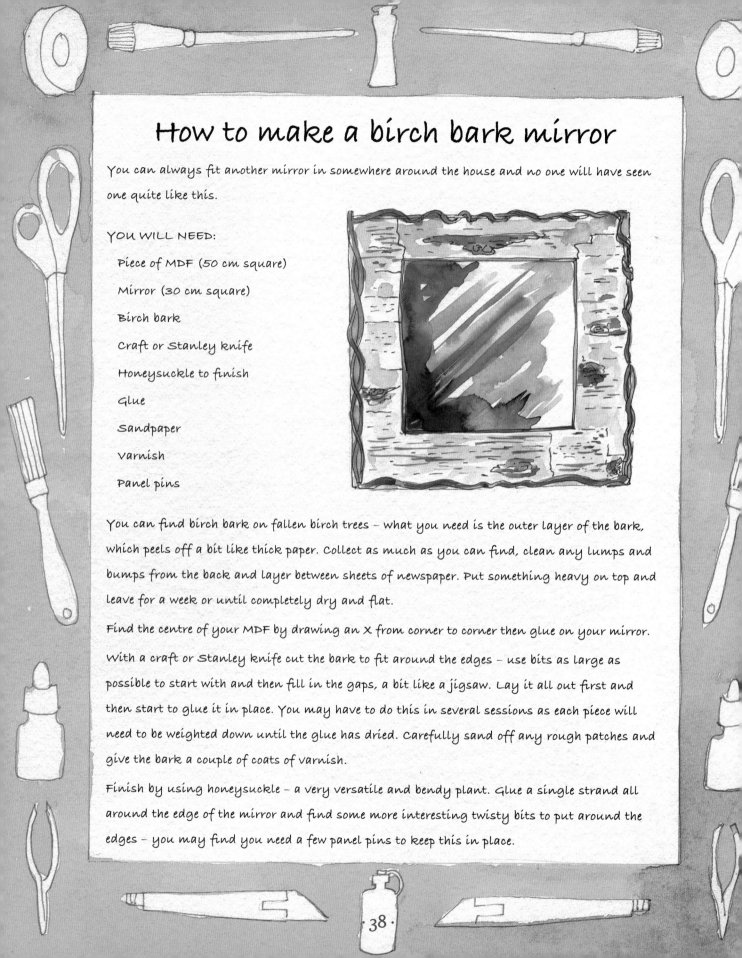

You can find birch bark on fallen birch trees – what you need is the outer layer of the bark, which peels off a bit like thick paper. Collect as much as you can find, clean any lumps and bumps from the back and layer between sheets of newspaper. Put something heavy on top and leave for a week or until completely dry and flat.

Find the centre of your MDF by drawing an X from corner to corner then glue on your mirror.

With a craft or Stanley knife cut the bark to fit around the edges – use bits as large as possible to start with and then fill in the gaps, a bit like a jigsaw. Lay it all out first and then start to glue it in place. You may have to do this in several sessions as each piece will need to be weighted down until the glue has dried. Carefully sand off any rough patches and give the bark a couple of coats of varnish.

Finish by using honeysuckle – a very versatile and bendy plant. Glue a single strand all around the edge of the mirror and find some more interesting twisty bits to put around the edges – you may find you need a few panel pins to keep this in place.

Is it a rabbit or a hare?

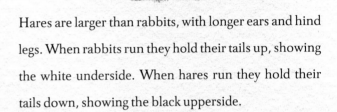

Hare

Rabbits live in burrows and give birth underground in nests lined with soft grasses and the mother's own fur – baby rabbits are called kittens. Hares live above ground and give birth in shallow depressions in the grass called 'forms'. Their young are called leverets.

Baby rabbits are born naked, helpless and unable to see whereas leverets are born fully furred and able to see – in fact a leveret is able to fend for itself from the moment it is born.

Rabbits are social animals and live in colonies known as warrens, whereas hares live mostly alone.

But both rabbits and hares have eyes at the sides of their heads so they can see behind without turning around.

Hares are larger than rabbits, with longer ears and hind legs. When rabbits run they hold their tails up, showing the white underside. When hares run they hold their tails down, showing the black upperside.

People talk about mad March hares – they aren't mad of course, but the sight of them leaping and dancing and apparently holding boxing matches makes them look as if they're going that way. What's actually happening is the unreceptive females seeing off amorous males until they are ready to mate.

Rabbit

Hare

March

· 39 ·

Is it a frog or a toad?

Toad

Frog

Probably the best way of telling a **frog** (*Rana temporaria*) from a **toad** (*Bufo bufo*) is by their skin – frogs have smooth, slimy skin whereas toads have a dry, warty skin. Their legs also differ – frogs have strong back legs and webbed feet for hopping and swimming; toads have short back legs because they tend to walk, not hop.

Frogs have more bulging eyes than toads and can lighten or darken their skin to suit their surroundings. They have a transparent inner eyelid to protect their eyes under water. Frogs tend to live in or near water, whereas toads only visit water to breed – in fact female toads return to the pond in which they were born to lay their spawn. Male frogs have nuptial pads on the first finger of their feet to grip females during mating.

Frog spawn and toad spawn are quite different to look at – frogs lay spawn in large clumps, while toad spawn is found in long strings. The eggs hatch into tadpoles (frogs) or toadpoles (toads), growing back legs before the front ones, before gradually absorbing their tails. Toadpoles are larger and rounder with blacker heads than tadpoles.

Toads are generally larger than frogs, with males reaching 8 cm long and females 13 cm. Male frogs are usually 6–8 cm long, and females 7–9 cm.

Frogs make easy prey, but toads have a parotoid gland behind their eye that produces a toxin (bufagin) – this makes them taste horrible and not at all attractive to most predators, although grass snakes and hedgehogs are immune to the toxin.

Both frogs and toads catch food with their long sticky tongues and eat invertebrates such as insects, larvae, spiders, slugs and worms. They hibernate from around October to January in muddy burrows or in mud at the bottom of ponds, or under layers of leaves.

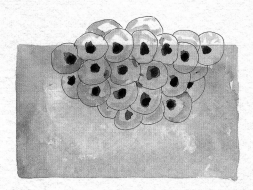

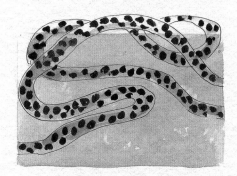

Frog spawn

Toad spawn

Freshwater Mussel

This Freshwater Mussel (*Unio tumidus*) was found in a wood a few hundred yards from a pond. This probably means it was eaten by a heron, although these mussels are also a favourite food of otters.

A bivalve that inhabits fresh water such as slow-moving rivers, lakes and ponds and particularly canals. The mussel is very sensitive to pollution so its presence is a good indicator that surrounding land is free from chemicals. The female mussel is fertilised by the male and can lay up to 200,000 eggs per year. She incubates the eggs for 4–6 weeks until the larvae hatch and then they live in fish gills for a few further weeks until they drop off and live in mud under water. Mussels are very long lived and although not poisonous are mostly too tough to eat.

Kingfisher

The most you'll probably see of this gorgeous little bird is an iridescent blue flash as it darts down a river or across a lake. But be patient and you may be lucky enough to spot a Kingfisher's (*Alcedo atthis*) regular perch, from where it sits and peers into the water waiting for a fish to pass by. When it sees one it dives straight in and returns to the perch with the fish in its mouth, whacking it on the branch to kill it before swallowing it head first.

Breeding takes place in holes dug in steep banks, using the bill rather than claws to dig. The female lays between six and eight eggs, both parents feed the young and they may have a second brood.

Dipper

Dippers (*Cinclus cinclus*) are one of the easiest birds to recognise as they are usually seen on a rock in fast-running water, bobbing up and down, sometimes described as curtseying. The bird walks into and under water searching for its food of aquatic crustaceans, molluscs and insects and can also be seen swimming and diving. It will have established a favourite beat and defend it from all comers.

The nests are always close to water and the cock bird helps build the nest, and incubate and feed the young.

Stag beetle

The stag beetle *Lucanus cervus* is the UK's largest beetle, whose branching jaws look like antlers and so give it its name.

- The antlers are used for fighting over territories and food.

- Broadleaved woodland is its preferred habitat.

- Eggs are laid between the end of May and beginning of August in rotting wood.

- Larvae spend up to 5 years underground feeding on rotting wood. This is not a very nutritious food, which is why they spend such a long time in this state.

- The larvae are C-shaped, with a pale-coloured body, six orange legs and an orange head and dark brown pincers.

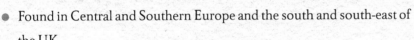

- Males emerge first.

- Fighting continues until one beetle turns the other over and the loser retreats – this is more a test of strength, and the beetles very rarely sustain any injury.

- Found in Central and Southern Europe and the south and south-east of the UK.

March flowers

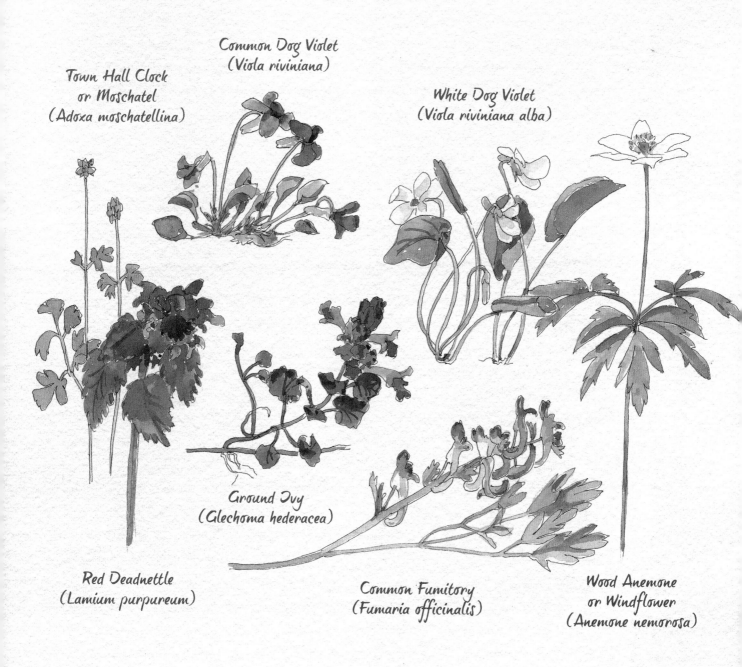

Town Hall Clock
or Moschatel
(Adoxa moschatellina)

Common Dog Violet
(Viola riviniana)

White Dog Violet
(Viola riviniana alba)

Ground Ivy
(Glechoma hederacea)

Red Deadnettle
(Lamium purpureum)

Common Fumitory
(Fumaria officinalis)

Wood Anemone
or Windflower
(Anemone nemorosa)

Mallard

The Mallard (*Anas platyrhynchos*) is possibly the most common and wide-ranging duck on the planet and the beautiful beetle-green shiny head of the male will be familiar to most people. They are omnivores and dabble for their food as well as graze. These ducks pair up in autumn and the drake will hang around until he's sure the ducklings have hatched and there is no hope or need of further mating. He will leave the female to do all the work, commence his moult and join up with other drakes.

Mallards nest on the ground in a well-hidden spot lined with grass and down, however as they now also live quite happily in cities they can sometimes lay their eggs in the most extraordinary places, such as high-up window boxes (the young will simply float down to earth as a downy ball as soon as they have hatched and dried) or in courtyards where the only way to leave is through the building. The duck will lay a clutch of around a dozen eggs and once this is complete she will start to incubate. The eggs will take approximately 28 days to hatch. The ducklings are precocial, meaning they can walk, feed and swim as soon as they hatch. The mother will lead them to water, which may be some distance away – a very dangerous time for a day-old duckling.

Once they reach water there are still terrors lurking beneath as pike in particular are very partial to young ducklings. They will stay with their mother for at least 2 months, following her as she emits the well-known 'quack-quack' call that can be heard for over a mile – the male's call is a more reedy quack that doesn't carry in the same way.

March

RECEIPE

Crystallised violets and primroses

Here is something really unusual to decorate your puddings or cakes. Preparing these is a rather fiddly process but well worth the trouble in the end.

First find your violets and primroses and pick them with their stalks on. Spread your picking about – don't pick every single flower from each plant.

YOU WILL NEED:

   Bunch of violets
   Bunch of primroses
   Icing sugar in a bowl
   One egg white
   Few drops of water

Whisk the egg white with a few drops of water until it just begins to froth.

Holding a flower by its stalk, dunk it gently in the egg white.

Dip it carefully into the icing sugar and make sure it is totally coated – sprinkle some on the back with your fingers.

If the petals curl up, uncurl them with a cocktail stick and place the flower on a rack covered in non-stick baking parchment.

Leave until totally dry – at least overnight, or put the rack in a very low oven or on top of an Aga.

Sprinkle a little more icing sugar on the flowers, snip off the stalks and place them carefully in a tin with sheets of non-stick baking parchment between layers.

Silver Birch

TYPE *Betula pendula* is a graceful deciduous woodland tree sometimes known as 'the shining one' because of its beautiful silvery bark.

SIZE The birch is what is called a 'pioneer tree', which colonises open ground and grows fast. It can reach heights of 30 m but is short-lived, surviving only 60–90 years.

BARK The bark in young trees is reddish-brown; it turns white with black patches as it matures. It shows yet another colour in spring when the twigs and buds have a characteristic purple colour, particularly when wet.

FOLIAGE The foliage of the Silver Birch is light and airy, with leaves that are triangular in shape with 'double teeth' (the teeth have teeth) up straight sides. Leaves are pale green but turn golden-yellow in autumn.

FRUIT It is monoecious, meaning that it produces both male and female flowers, the male a drooping catkin that produces pollen in the spring and the female, a smaller upright one. Pollinated by the wind, the female catkin ripens into longer hanging tails in late summer, producing seeds that have two tiny transparent wings – each tree can produce up to one million.

USES The bark of the birch is remarkably versatile. Rolled up it can be used as a torch due to the presence of volatile oil. In the past the white epidermis was used for a wide variety of things such as baskets, plates, roofing material and even footwear. A slice placed in the sole of a boot acts as a foot warmer. In the northern USA the skin of the birch was used to make the canoes of the native tribes.

March

April

The 1st of April some do say
Is set apart for All Fools' Day
But why the people call it so
Not I, nor they themselves do know

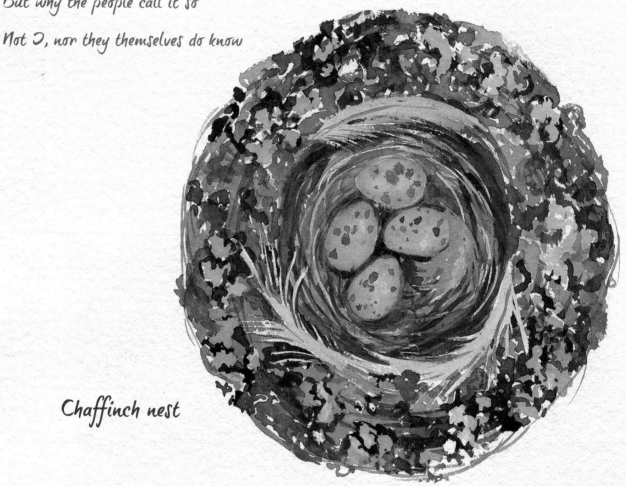

Chaffinch nest

Calmer, longer and warmer days mean growth can really start and there will be plenty of flowers in the woods and hedgerows. The dawn chorus will be in full flow as birds are mating and nesting. It is important that it's warm enough for insect caterpillars to be hatching or the hardworking adults won't be able to feed their young. Inexperienced nesters will soon be discovered by Magpies and Jays and have to start again.

This is the month to listen out for the Cuckoo, who arrives on our shores with remarkable regularity, although it has no idea what the weather will be like when it leaves its African wintering grounds. Swallows and Swifts will also have made their huge journeys, but some birds such as geese and swans will leave the UK for their summer breeding territories in Northern Europe and even within the Arctic Circle.

April

Who ate the egg?

At this time of year you can often find an eggshell, or part of an eggshell, lying on the ground. Once their chicks are hatched, nesting birds remove eggs from their nests, sometimes fitting one half into the other to save a journey, and drop them well away from the nest so as not to attract inquisitive magpies or other predators. If an egg has been eaten by a predator it is possible to work out who the villain was by looking carefully at it. A naturally hatched egg will be broken into two halves and the membrane may be visible. If the egg is mainly whole and the little bits of loose shell around the hole lean inwards and traces of yolk or blood are in evidence, then someone has eaten this egg. Look to see whether there are punched tooth marks or if just the end has been bitten off – in which case the culprit is a fox. If there are scratches, these are more likely to have been made by a beak, and it was probably a Magpie, crow or Jay that ate the egg.

Thrush nest

Common birds' eggs

Great Spotted
Woodpecker

Skylark

Swallow

House
Martin

Grey Wagtail

Dunnock

Spotted
Flycatcher

Chiffchaff

Robin

Fieldfare

Blue Tit

Blackbird

Song
Thrush

House Sparrow

Chaffinch

Starling

Jay

Jackdaw

Wren

Greater Black-backed Gull

Guillemot

Cormorant

Greenshank

Grey Heron

Tawny Owl

Kestrel

Buzzard

April

Cuckoo

The Cuckoo (*Cuculus canorus*) is one of the wonders of the bird world, managing to parasitise the nests of other birds and leave the usually diminutive owners to bring up their young for them.

- The Cuckoo's name is onomatopoeic (that is, its call sounds like its name).
- Cuckoos spend most of their time in Africa, where they never call.
- Only the male calls 'cuckoo' – the female has a quieter bubbling call.
- The female lays two clutches of 5–7 eggs, all in different nests.
- Her favourite hosts are Dunnock, Meadow Pipit, Reed Bunting and Pied Wagtail.
- She usually lays in nests of the breed that reared her and her eggs resemble those of the host.
- Around 20% of eggs are rejected by suspicious hosts.

- She usually lays in the afternoon, carefully watching for the host to leave the nest, then ejecting an egg and laying her own all in about 10 seconds.

- When the Cuckoo chick hatches it pushes all other chicks and eggs out of the nest.

- The chick makes a cheeping sound that fools the host into thinking it has a nest full of young.

- Adult Cuckoos return to Africa as soon as the breeding season is over, sometimes as early as the end of June.

- Fledged Cuckoos follow their parents around the end of September.

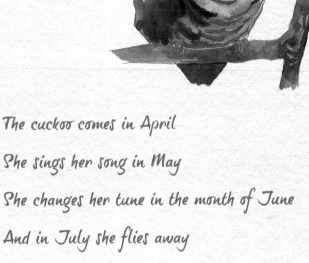

The cuckoo comes in April

She sings her song in May

She changes her tune in the month of June

And in July she flies away

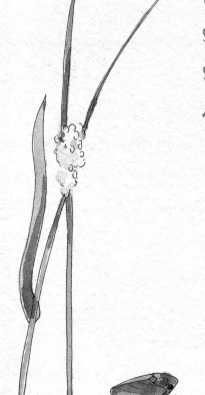

Cuckoo spit

Cuckoo spit has nothing to do with Cuckoos, apart from the fact that it appears at the same time as the Cuckoo. It is in fact a frothy liquid produced by immature nymphs of a froghopper to protect it from predators. Inside the spit is a little sap-eating creature that has a very vague resemblance to a baby frog. Once it becomes adult it leaves its frothy home and uses its amazing ability to jump to keep it out of danger. For its size and weight it can jump even further than a flea.

April

How to make honeysuckle cutlery

With a little ingenuity you can make something totally unique that is actually useful. What you need are bits of wood or honeysuckle that will make handles – the actual spoon or blade you will have to buy, but you can get these from woodturning suppliers.

YOU WILL NEED:

Small saw

Sandpaper

Drill

Strong wood glue

Varnish

Salad server, spoon, cheese knife or cake slice blank

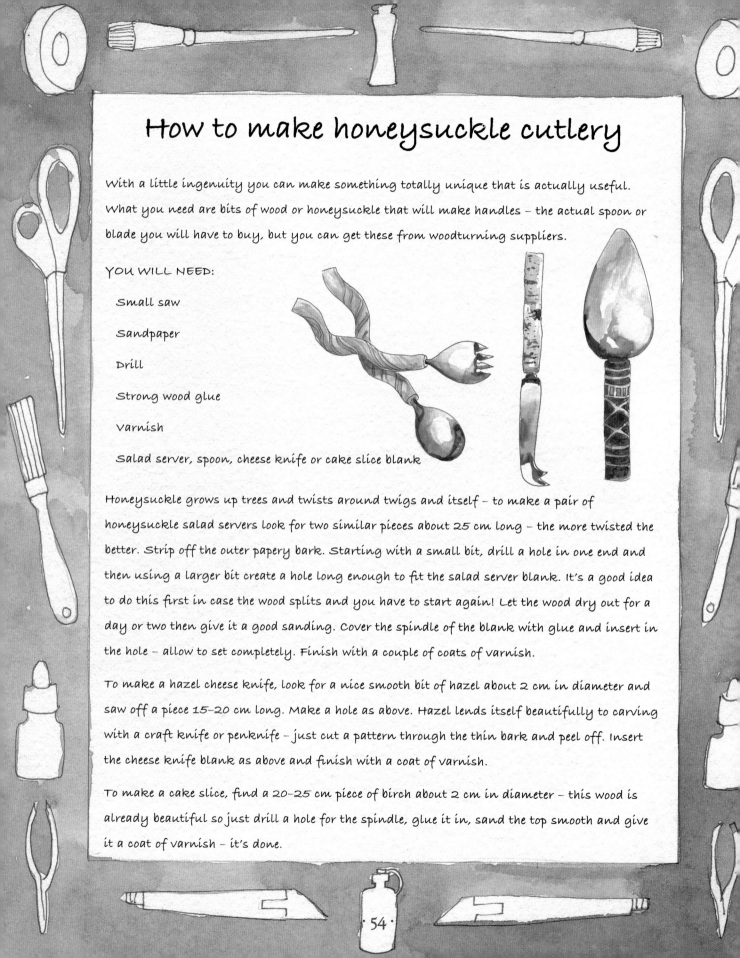

Honeysuckle grows up trees and twists around twigs and itself – to make a pair of honeysuckle salad servers look for two similar pieces about 25 cm long – the more twisted the better. Strip off the outer papery bark. Starting with a small bit, drill a hole in one end and then using a larger bit create a hole long enough to fit the salad server blank. It's a good idea to do this first in case the wood splits and you have to start again! Let the wood dry out for a day or two then give it a good sanding. Cover the spindle of the blank with glue and insert in the hole – allow to set completely. Finish with a couple of coats of varnish.

To make a hazel cheese knife, look for a nice smooth bit of hazel about 2 cm in diameter and saw off a piece 15–20 cm long. Make a hole as above. Hazel lends itself beautifully to carving with a craft knife or penknife – just cut a pattern through the thin bark and peel off. Insert the cheese knife blank as above and finish with a coat of varnish.

To make a cake slice, find a 20–25 cm piece of birch about 2 cm in diameter – this wood is already beautiful so just drill a hole for the spindle, glue it in, sand the top smooth and give it a coat of varnish – it's done.

Bumblebees

- There are around 250 types of bumblebees in the world, 19 in the UK and 66 in Europe.

- Bumblebees only produce just enough honey to feed their young.

- The queen starts a new nest off with about six eggs in a ball of pollen, the grubs eat this until they pupate and eventually hatch into worker bees who then support the queen as she continues to lay.

- When the nest has reached the correct number for the species the queen lays eggs that will become the following year's queens, as well as male bees or drones.

- The drones leave the nest, their only purpose in life being to mate with young queens.

- Drones have no sting.

- Unlike honey bees, female bumblebees do not lose their sting and die if they use it.

- In the autumn the old queen, her worker bees and the drones will die, leaving the newly mated young queens to hibernate and start again in the spring.

- Bumblebees are not aggressive and do not attack humans.

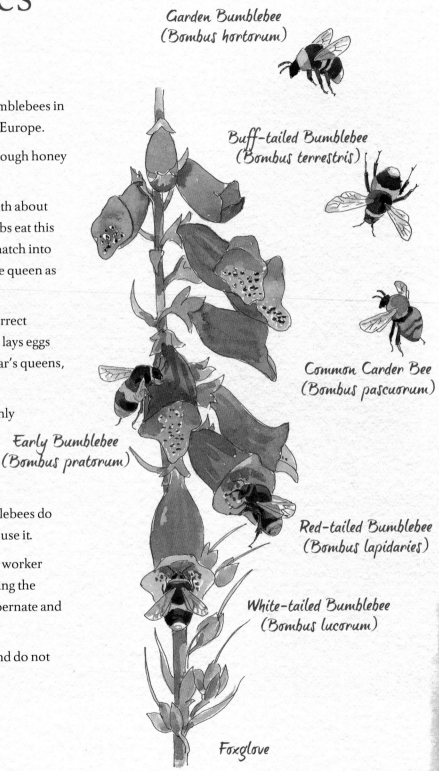

Garden Bumblebee
(Bombus hortorum)

Buff-tailed Bumblebee
(Bombus terrestris)

Common Carder Bee
(Bombus pascuorum)

Early Bumblebee
(Bombus pratorum)

Red-tailed Bumblebee
(Bombus lapidaries)

White-tailed Bumblebee
(Bombus lucorum)

Foxglove

April

April flowers

Yellow Archangel
(Galeobdolon luteum)

Bluebell
(Endymion non-scriptus)

Bugle
(Ajuga reptans)

Forget-me-not
(Myosotis arvensis)

Petty Spurge
(Euphorbia peplus)

Wood Spurge
(Euphorbia
amygdaloides)

Ransoms or
Wild Garlic
(Allium ursinum)

Cuckoo Flower
or Lady's Smock
(Cardamine pratensis)

White Dead-nettle
(Lamium album)

April

Hedgehog

Hedgehogs (*Erinaceus europaeus*) can grow to 25 cm in length and weigh about 1 kg fully grown. They hibernate in the winter, depending on the year from November to March, and are also nocturnal. As they hunt they make a sort of grunting noise, a little like a pig – hence their name.

Hedgehogs are covered in spines, around 5,000 of them, and they harbour a specific species of flea. The spines are the hedgehog's protection but they also have the ability to curl up into a tight ball so that the spines stick out in every direction and it would take a very determined predator to break through this prickly wall. Often called the gardener's friend for their habit of eating slugs, snails, caterpillars and insects, they also eat worms and the eggs of ground-nesting birds – and can become a serious threat to such birds where they have been introduced, such as to the Hebridean Islands.

Baby hedgehogs are called hoglets, adult females are sows and males are boars. Litters of up to five hoglets are born from May onwards. They are born blind, with their spines just below the skin, but after 2 weeks their eyes open and the spines appear.

Surprisingly hedgehogs can swim and are also good climbers – quite capable of scaling stone walls.

Slugs

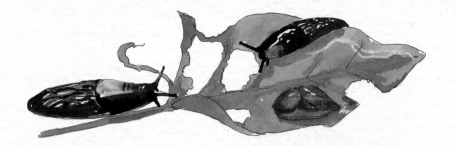

There are about 30 different species of slug in the UK, varying in colour from bright orange to black. They can be up to 16 cm long, the largest being the Leopard Slug (*Limax maximus*), which feeds on mould and rotting wood rather than plants.

- Slugs are around from April to November and favour damp warm weather.

- In winter they hibernate under logs or anything they can find and may even choose to come into your house.

- They are related to snails but lack the shell, having instead a leathery patch on their backs called a mantle shield. This has a hole in it which is the slug's nostril.

- Slugs exude a slime that lubricates their movement and helps to stop them from drying out – if you get some on your hands it is remarkably difficult to get off but rubbing on a dry towel will be more successful than trying to wash it off with water. It also acts as a deterrent to predators and contains a mild anaesthetic.

- Slugs are hermaphroditic.

- A slug's mouth is on its underside and contains a radula, a sort of rasping tongue.

Swift, Swallow or Martin?

Swifts (*Apus apus*) are dark sooty brown with a pale throat but appear black against the sky. The tail is slightly forked, although less so than a Swallow. They fly low and fast, screaming as they go. Swifts never perch because they have tiny legs and can hardly walk. They drink, feed, preen and even sleep on the wing, and nest in holes.

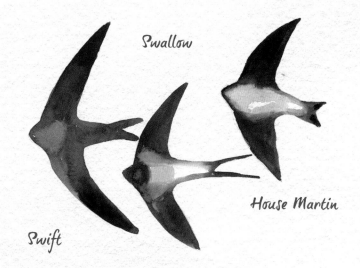

Swallow

Swift

House Martin

Swallows (*Hirundo rustica*) are dark glossy blue-black backs, wings and heads with a reddish patch on the chin and upper throat, and cream underparts. Their long forked tails are distinctive – the males have a longer tail than the females. Swallows are often seen swooping low over water catching insects or perching on wires, when you can hear their twittery voices. They nest mainly in buildings, building a nest cup from mud and straw.

House Martins (*Delichon urbica*) also have a forked tail but it is shorter than that of the Swallow. They have glossy blue upperparts, are white underneath and have a distinctive white rump. Like Swallows, they can often be seen swooping over water and flying low to catch insects. They have a twittering song but also a sharp chirrup. Their nests are mud cups under the eaves of houses.

Two swallows do not make a summer

When the swallows fly high
The weather will be dry

Sand Martins (*Riparia riparia*) are similar in shape to House Martins, but have earthy brown backs, with a brown breast band and white underside. Their voice is similar to that of the Swallow and House Martin but they are generally quieter. They live in colonies so are usually seen in groups and their nests consist of burrows in sandy river banks, quarries or cliffs.

April

RECESPE

Wild garlic pesto

This makes one of the most unusual additions to pasta or anything you might add normal pesto to – you can even spread it on toast. Pick the leaves tactfully, spreading your picking and not simply taking every leaf from the nearest plants.

YOU WILL NEED:

100 g wild garlic leaves

50 g Parmesan, grated

50 g pine nuts

150 ml olive oil

Salt and pepper to taste

Wash the wild garlic leaves and dry them carefully.

Add all the ingredients to a food mixer and whizz until smooth.

Check seasoning and adjust if necessary.

Tip into sterilised jars, cover and keep in the fridge or a cool dark place. It will keep in the fridge for 2–3 weeks.

English Oak

TYPE *Quercus robur* is a long-lived deciduous broadleaf tree. It is not unknown for oaks to live 500 years or more, indeed Old Knobbley of Essex is thought to be as much as 800 years old. Oaks support more wildlife in their branches than any other British tree – including up to 284 species of insect.

SIZE 15–25 m.

BARK Grey with knobbly ridges and brown twigs, particularly attractive to lichens.

FOLIAGE Leaves are lobed and arranged alternately on the twig. Twigs bear catkins in May.

FRUIT Male and female flowers are produced. The male flowers are the catkins and the female flowers are tiny and found in the axils of the leaves. When fertilised they turn into acorns and are attached to a peduncle. One to four acorns are attached to each peduncle. Trees do not produce acorns until they are around 40 years old.

USES Excellent timber once used for boat building and still used in the building of houses. The bark is used in the tanning of leather. Acorns are much prized for fattening pigs. The wood also makes good firewood and is used by the Druids for their ceremonial fires – druid meaning 'oak man'.

April

May

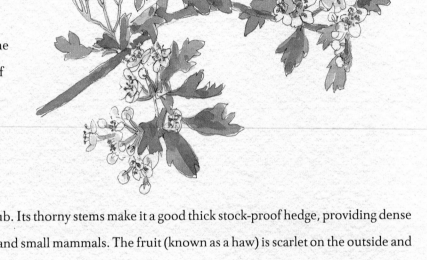

Rather than referring to the month of May, the above saying refers to the shrubby tree and warns us not to think summer has arrived or to put our vests away just yet!

Spring has officially arrived and with the blossom come the Bullfinches, lovers of buds, especially those of the Hawthorn (*Crataegus monogyna*).

Also known as May (as it generally flowers during the month of May), Hawthorn is a common hedgerow shrub. Its thorny stems make it a good thick stock-proof hedge, providing dense cover and protection for nesting birds and small mammals. The fruit (known as a haw) is scarlet on the outside and yellow and pithy on the inside.

This shrub has many medicinal uses as well as being edible – young leaves and buds can be added to salads, and the berries and flowers made into teas and jelly. The wood can be used for engraver's blocks and the wood from the roots was once used to make combs.

Many myths are associated with the Hawthorn – its blossoms were used for garlands on May Day. It was connected with fertility and produced at weddings; its protective charms against evil, witches, vampires and lightning meant that houses and particularly wells would have a Hawthorn growing nearby. It's considered unlucky to bring Hawthorn into the house – once thought to invite death, this is more likely to be because the blossom has the unpleasant smell of decomposing flesh.

At the same time as the Hawthorn is flowering the Hawthorn or St Mark's Fly (*Bibio marci*) is flying. You can easily recognise this large fly by its dangling legs. There are often swarms of males in the air looking for the females on the ground – as soon as a female takes off it is seized upon by the males and mating takes place in the air.

May

Is it a mayfly or a maybug?

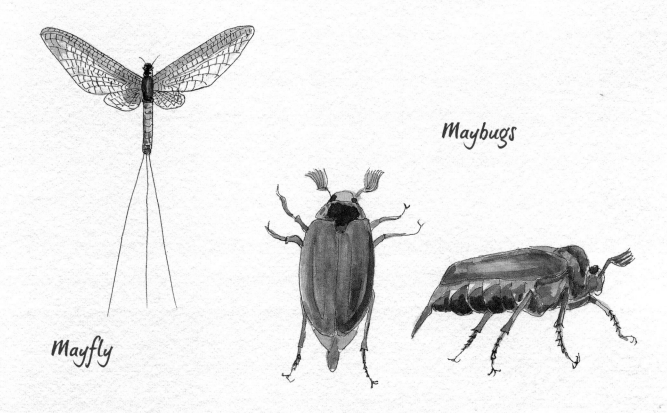

Maybugs

Mayfly

There are many different members of the Ephemeroptera (from Greek, meaning 'lives for a day') family and not all hatch in May. *Ephemera danica* (above left) is one of the largest **Mayflies** and also the one that fishermen (and fish!) delight in when they hatch in huge numbers during May.

Mayflies lay their eggs in or on fresh water and the larvae or nymphs live in the water. They may remain in this state for up to two years but when ready to emerge they come to the surface and shed their skin. Unique to mayflies is the fact that they shed their skins once

more before they are able to fly properly. Adults mate on the wing, do not eat, lay their eggs and die.

The **Maybug or Cockchafer** (*Melolontha melolontha*) (above right) is a large, noisy and rather clumsy insect that times its hatching to May. The male is distinguished from the female by its fan-like antennae. Maybugs lie up during the day and fly at night, visiting flowers. They are attracted to light and are a common indoor visitor. The chafer larvae live for several years underground, consuming roots and if found in large numbers can do serious damage to grasses and crops.

Greater Celandine

The Greater Celandine (*Chelidonium majus*) is a remarkable plant that seems to cure all ills. It has been used since Roman times – in particular the leaves and sap can be used to remove warts. However it is thought to cure a whole host of other things, both internally and externally, including bronchitis, asthma, jaundice, cancer, cataracts and corns – but care should be taken if self-medicating as the yellow-orange sap is in fact toxic.

The Latin name *Chelidonium* derives from the Greek 'chelidon' (meaning 'swallow'), because the flowers appear at the same time as the swallows arrive. A member of the *Papaveraceae* or poppy family, it bears no relation to the Lesser Celandine.

Take ooze of this same wort or the blossoms wrung out, and mixed with honey; mingle them gently hot ashes thereto, and seethe together in a brazen vessell; this is a special leechdom for dimness of eyes.

Herbarium, 5th century

May

White butterflies

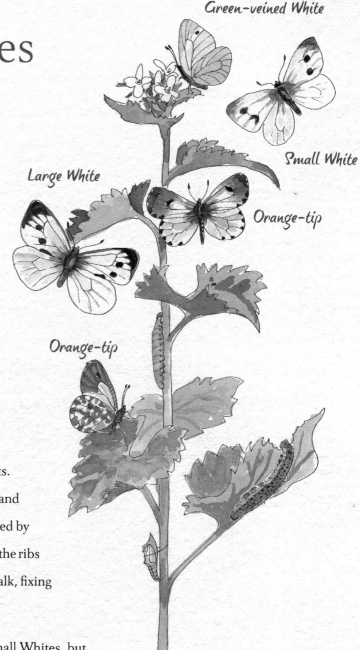

Green-veined White

Small White

Large White

Orange-tip

Orange-tip

The larvae of **Large Whites** (*Pieris brassicae*) gorge on the cabbages in your veg patch, but also feed on any plants of the Cruciferae family. Eggs are laid in groups on the underside of leaves and young larvae stay together until the first moult when they form a line along the edge of a leaf, devouring it as they move backwards. They pupate attached to leaves or stems or even crawl away and fix themselves to tree trunks or fences. Many fall prey to the parasitic ichneumon fly that lays its eggs in the body of the caterpillar, eventually killing it.

Small Whites (*Pieris rapae*) also love cruciferous plants. Females lay eggs on the underside of leaves singly and over a wide area. The well camouflaged caterpillars feed by making holes in a leaf; when not feeding they lie along the ribs of the leaf. They pupate in an upright position on a stalk, fixing themselves to it with a silken girdle.

Green-veined Whites (*Pieris napi*) look similar to Small Whites, but have more pronounced veins on the underside of the wings, and also feed on cruciferous plants. The female lays eggs singly and when the caterpillar hatches it makes a hole through a leaf to start feeding immediately.

Only the male **Orange-tip** (*Anthocharis cardamines*) lives up to its name, the female has a black spot on each forewing; both sexes are mottled on the undersides of the wings. Females lay a single egg on the flowers of cruciferous plants, the egg turns from white through bright orange to dark grey. Once hatched the caterpillars feed on seed pods rather than leaves. This particular larva is also a cannibal, attacking and eating its own kind.

A beetle of beetles

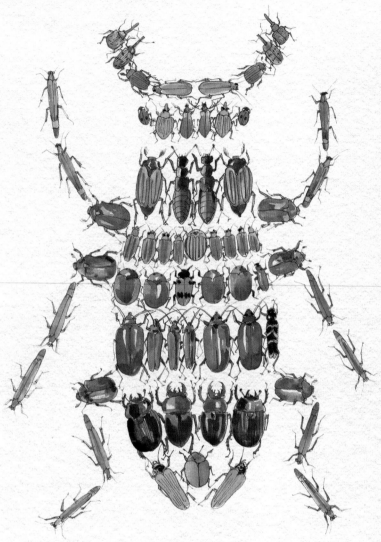

1. *Caenorhinus aequatus*
2. *Dorytomus longimanus* (f)
3. Garden Chafer (*Phyllopertha horticola*)
4. Soldier Beetle (*Rhagonycha fulva*)
5. Two-spot Ladybird (*Adalia bipunctata*)
6. *Apion miniatum*
7. Cardinal Beetle (*Pyrochroa coccinea*)
8. *Lymexlon navale* (f)
9. Common Cockchafer (*Melolontha melolontha*)
10. Devil's Coach Horse (*Ocypus olens*)
11. Rose Chafer (*Cetonia aurata*)

12. *Donacia vulgaris*
13. Colorado Beetle (*Leptinotarsa decemlineata*)
14. *Lema melanopa*
15. *Chrysolina hyperici*
16. *Clytra quadripunctata*
17. Wasp Beetle (*Clytus arietis*)
18. Longhorn Beetle (*Prionus coriarius*)
19. *Aromia moschata*
20. Dor Beetle (*Geotrupes stercorarius*)
21. Stag Beetle (*Lucanus cervus*)
22. Tortoise Beetle (*Cassida viridis*)
23. *Cebrio gigas*

May

Is it an Adder, Grass Snake or Slow Worm?

The **Adder** (*Vipera berus*) and the **Grass Snake** (*Natrix natirx*) are often confused, but there are some crucial differences between them, which are important because while Grass Snakes are harmless, Adders are venomous. The most significant difference is that Adders have a marked 'V' on the back of their heads and a zigzag pattern along the back. Adders can vary in colour but the male is usually darker than the female. Grass Snakes are olive green or brownish with a pale yellow and black collar. They can reach up to 120 cm in length whereas adders generally only reach 60 cm.

Adders have a broad angular head with a reddish eye and vertical pupil – Grass Snakes have a more elegant head with a round pupil. Both shed their skin at least once a year.

Adder

Grass Snake

Slow Worm

Adders feed on voles, mice, lizards, nestlings and eggs, while Grass Snakes feed on frogs, toads, small rodents and eggs. Grass Snakes swallow their prey head first, usually alive, while the Adder injects its prey with venom and waits for it to die before eating it.

Adder

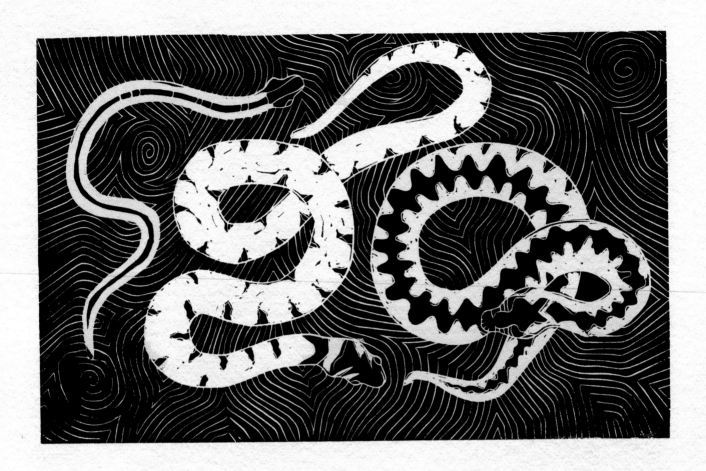

Grass Snakes are good swimmers and often live near water, in damp meadows or woodland. Adders prefer to live on dry heathland and moors. They both hibernate between October and March.

Adders give birth to live young that form inside the mother's body from eggs between July and September. Grass Snakes lay eggs in rotting vegetation or where there is warmth, such as in a compost heap. The eggs hatch in August and September.

The **Slow Worm** (*Anguis fragilis*) is in fact a legless lizard and not a snake at all. It has smooth shiny pale bronze skin with a stripe down the middle. They can be up to 45 cm long, but are usually smaller. Slow Worms are able to close their eyes, unlike snakes which can't. They feed on slugs, snails and insects and are able to shed their tails if attacked (known as autotomy), the idea being that the tail continues to wriggle, distracting the predator while the lizard makes its escape.

May

May flowers

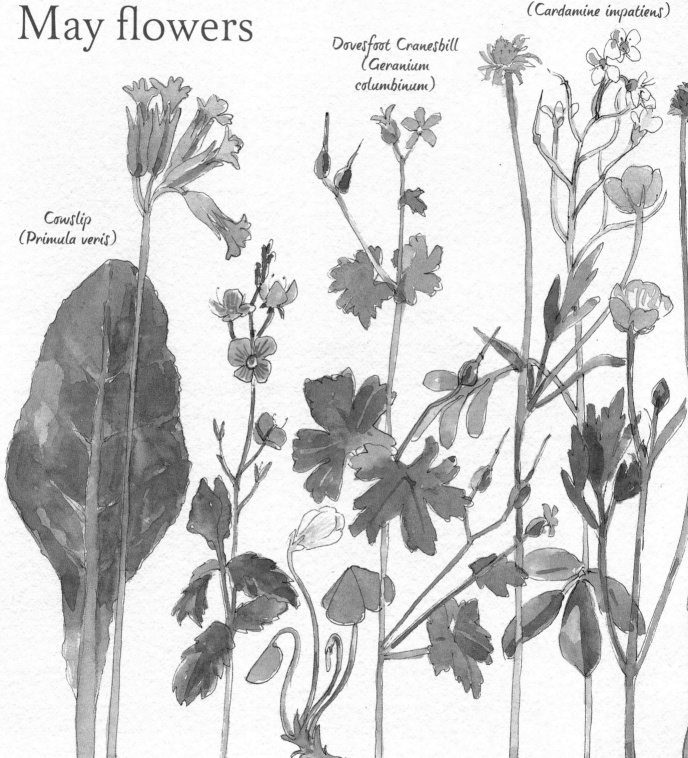

Cowslip
(Primula veris)

Dovesfoot Cranesbill
(Geranium
columbinum)

Bitter Cress
(Cardamine impatiens)

Germander Speedwell
(Veronica chamaedrys)

Wood Sorrel
(Oxalis acetocella)

Buttercup
(Ranunculus acris)

Ground Ivy
(Glechoma hederacea)

Common Speedwell
(Veronica officinalis)

Herb Robert
(Geranium robertianum)

Sheep's Sorrel
(Rumex acetosella)

Hop Trefoil
(Trifolium campestre)

Yellow Pimpernel
(Lysimachia nemorum)

Lesser Stitchwort
(Stellaria graminea)

Field Pansy
(Viola arvensis)

May

· 73 ·

Garden Snail

The garden snail (*Helix aspersa*) has been around for 60 million years.

- The snail's slime acts as suction so that they can hang upside down.

- Snails are hermaphroditic and although they can self-fertilise they usually mate. They caress each other with their tentacles then pierce each other's shell with a calcareous 'love-dart'. After fertilisation both will produce eggs that are laid in the soil.

- They are nocturnal but will come out during the day after rain.

- Snails cannot tolerate salt.

- A broth made from snail's mucus was once used to treat sore throats.

- After 2 weeks around 80 eggs are laid in topsoil and up to six batches can be laid in one year.

- An adult's shell has four or five whorls, but every shell is different in colour and design.

- The entire body can be retracted into the shell and sealed in with a thin membrane of mucus (called an epiphragm) that keeps their body moist when hibernating.

- During hibernation they prevent themselves freezing by altering the osmotic components of their blood.

- The head has four tentacles, the upper two with eye-like sensors and the lower two with tactile feelers that can be retracted into the head.

- The garden snail is a herbivore.

- The muscular foot secretes mucus to enable the snail to move and its top speed is 1.3cm per second.

- Garden snails are edible.

Leaf shapes

Cordate

Dentate

Digitate

Elliptic

Filiform

Hastate

Lanceolate

Lobate

Oblanceolate

Orbicular

Palmate

Peltate

Perfoliate

Pinnate

Pinnatifid

Rhomboidal

Sagittate

Spathulate

Trifoliate

Undulate

May

Emperor Moth

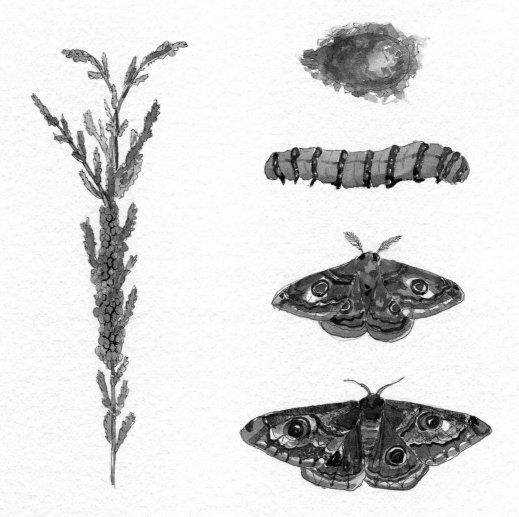

The beautiful Emperor Moth (*Saturnia pavonia*) is one that you just might see out on a walk, as the males fly during the day as they hunt for females. The females give off a pheromone that the males can pick up from as far as 3 km away. This moth is one of the largest moths found in the UK, the female being larger than the male.

Within a few hours of mating the female lays her eggs on the larval food plant of heather, bramble or sallow and when first hatched the caterpillars are black, but they soon become green with yellow, pink or white spots and black bristles.

When the caterpillars are ready to pupate they spin a large cocoon in which they overwinter, to emerge as adult moths in April or May. Emperors are the only UK member of the silk moth family.

Papier maché dock leaf dishes

Papier maché is a very versatile way of creating odd-shaped objects and is remarkably tough – the following method will make a fun dish for serving nuts or nibbles.

YOU WILL NEED:

A large dock (or other large) leaf

Newspaper

Cling film

Soft pastry brush

Small amount of tissue paper

Acrylic paint

Varnish

Papier maché glue

Flour and water (to make the glue)

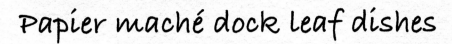

Make your glue in a ratio of 1 of flour to 4 of water. Put 3 teacupfuls of water into a pan and bring to the boil, meanwhile stir 1 teacupful of water into the flour and mix until smooth – pour it into the boiling water, stirring all the time, and boil for 2–3 minutes. Allow to cool. This will keep in the fridge for a couple of weeks, or even longer if you add a teaspoon of salt.

Find a large leaf – dock or burdock are ideal. Scrunch up some newspaper vaguely the size of the leaf and lay the leaf over this, letting the sides hang down to create a shallow bowl shape. Cover with cling film. Tear newspaper into 10 cm pieces, brush each with glue and stick them onto the leaf, painting more glue on the back and pressing into any nooks or crannies. Continue overlapping the pieces until the whole leaf has at least two layers. Don't worry about the edges yet. Allow to dry overnight in a warm place, then continue to add layers in the same way until at you have at least 10 and they are completely dry. Now lift up your creation, trim the sides and glue one or two layers of tissue paper over the raw edges – let this dry.

Paint with acrylic paint – any colour you fancy – and finish with two coats of varnish.

Ladybirds

Ladybirds belong to the Coccinellidae family and are in fact beetles belonging to the order *Coleoptera*.

There are around 40 different types of ladybird in the UK, although some would hardly be recognised as such. Some, like the common two-spot ladybird, come in a variety of different spot patterns and colours. Their bold colouring serves to warn birds that they are not good to eat. However, some birds like swifts and swallows that feed on the wing, are immune to the ladybird's defensive chemical. Ladybirds feed mainly on aphids and mildew and one ladybird can consume as many as 5,000 aphids in its lifetime.

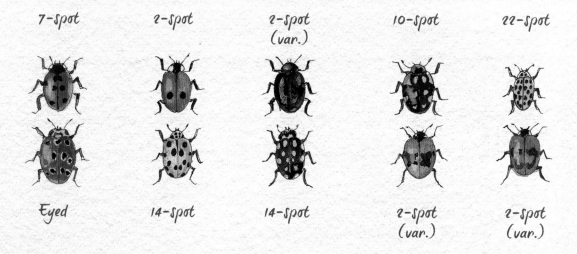

Ladybirds hibernate during the winter, tucking themselves into crevices in bark or rock, although they can often be seen in the cracks at the sides of windows. Eggs are laid in June to July, which hatch into larvae – little black grubs that also feed on aphids until they pupate. Hatching takes place in August but the young ladybirds do not mate until the following year.

Our native ladybirds are now under threat from a foreign invader known as a harlequin ladybird. Harlequins are very similar to native ladybirds and the best way to tell them apart is to look at the legs. Native ladybirds have black legs and harlequins brown. If the ladybird you are looking at is less than 5 mm in length then it is not a harlequin as they are generally larger.

Water voles

The water vole (*Arvicola amphibious*) is also known as the water rat (and is of course familiar as Ratty in *Wind in the Willows*).

- Water voles are semi-aquatic rodents and are protected in the UK as their numbers have fallen dramatically, thanks partly to the introduction of mink.

- Water voles can grow to 14–22 cm (5½ to 8½ in) in length but have a short lifespan, of less than 2 years.

- Males are slightly larger than females, except during pregnancy when the females become larger.

- They excavate extensive burrows in the banks of rivers, ponds and ditches.

- The burrows have underwater entrances and sleeping chambers.

- A vole will eat around 80% of its body weight every day.

- Waterside plants and grass are their main food.

- Voles can have up to five litters a year, of between three and seven young.

- They are territorial during breeding, leaving piles of green droppings known as latrines to mark their territory.

May

RECIPE

Elderflower cordial

A common hedgerow shrub, the elderflower comes into its own in May, when it produces its fragrant flower heads – delicious if cooked with gooseberries, but even better as a cordial to be diluted with plain or sparkling water. The cordial will keep for some weeks in the fridge but any excess is best frozen in plastic bottles.

YOU WILL NEED:

25 elderflower heads

1.5 kg sugar

4 lemons, sliced

50 g citric acid

1 litre boiling water

Place the elderflower heads, sugar, citric acid and lemons in a large bowl. Pour over the boiling water. Cover and leave for 24 hours. Sieve through muslin and bottle. What could be simpler?

Beech

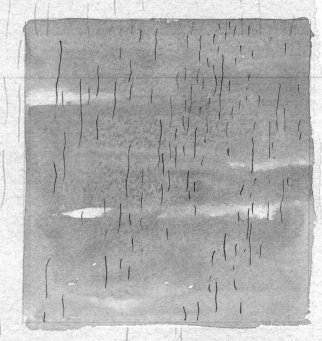

TYPE *Fagus sylvatica* is an elegant broadleaf deciduous tree that can live for 300 years. Also found in a copper form.

SIZE 25–35 m.

BARK Smooth, sleek light grey.

FOLIAGE Oval with 5–9 pairs of veins. Leaves arranged alternately along the twigs.

FRUIT Nuts known as beech mast that form inside green prickly husks that turn brown when ripe. Often a bumper crop forms every four or five years, known as 'mast years' and much appreciated by wildlife. Beech mast was once used to fatten pigs.

USES Furniture, in particular chairs made by 'bodgers', kitchen utensils and excellent firewood. Used to smoke herrings. Much prized as a hedge as it often retains its dead leaves over winter (marcescence), creating shelter.

June

If at dimpsey frogs be croakin',
we'em soon be due a soakin'

Make a daisy chain or ask the daisy
a question – foolish perhaps, as
you may get the wrong answer to
'he loves me, he loves me not'.

Poppies germinate best in disturbed ground, which is why they covered the fields of conflict in Flanders after the First World War with an amazing red carpet. June is a beautiful month, with the leaves on the trees still fresh and butterflies and insects on the wing. The midsummer solstice or longest day falls on 21 June, so days are long and nights are short.

Grass will be flowering and producing pollen and now is the time to take a wander after dark and see if you can spot an elusive glow worm with its astonishing neon light.

June

Orchids

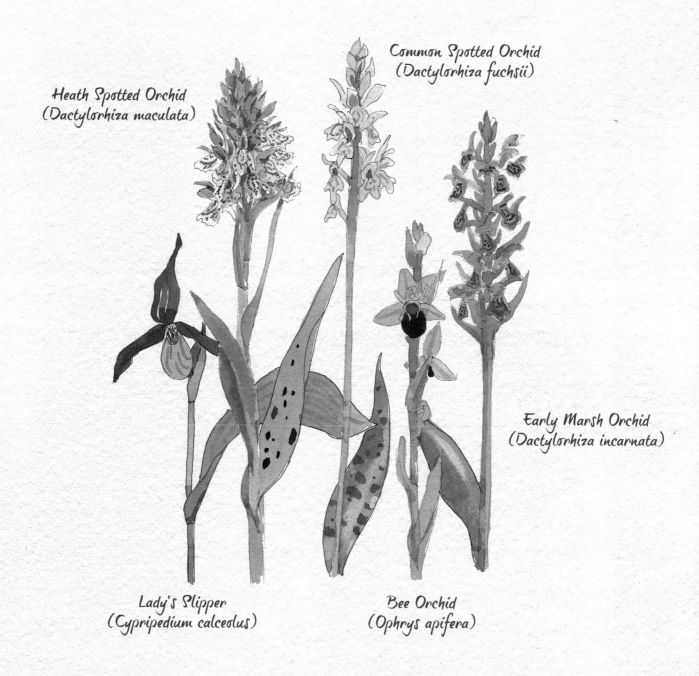

Heath Spotted Orchid
(Dactylorhiza maculata)

Common Spotted Orchid
(Dactylorhiza fuchsii)

Early Marsh Orchid
(Dactylorhiza incarnata)

Lady's Slipper
(Cypripedium calceolus)

Bee Orchid
(Ophrys apifera)

There's something exotic even about the word orchid, so finding one in the wild is always exciting. Unbelievably there are 56 varieties found in the UK, a handful of which are illustrated above, and many more in Europe. Some are very rare and others only grow in specific localities – all are protected and it is an offence to pick or uproot them.

Vetches

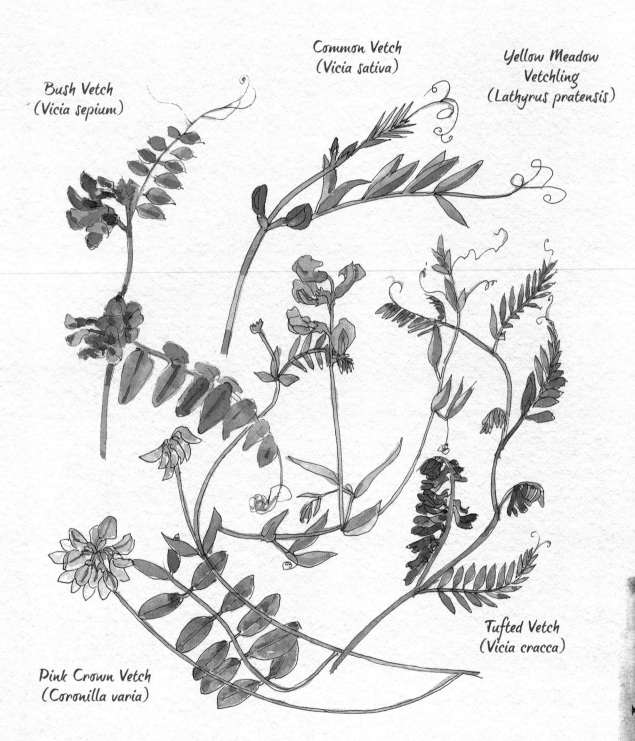

Bush Vetch
(Vicia sepium)

Common Vetch
(Vicia sativa)

Yellow Meadow
Vetchling
(Lathyrus pratensis)

Pink Crown Vetch
(Coronilla varia)

Tufted Vetch
(Vicia cracca)

June

Dragonflies on Yellow Iris

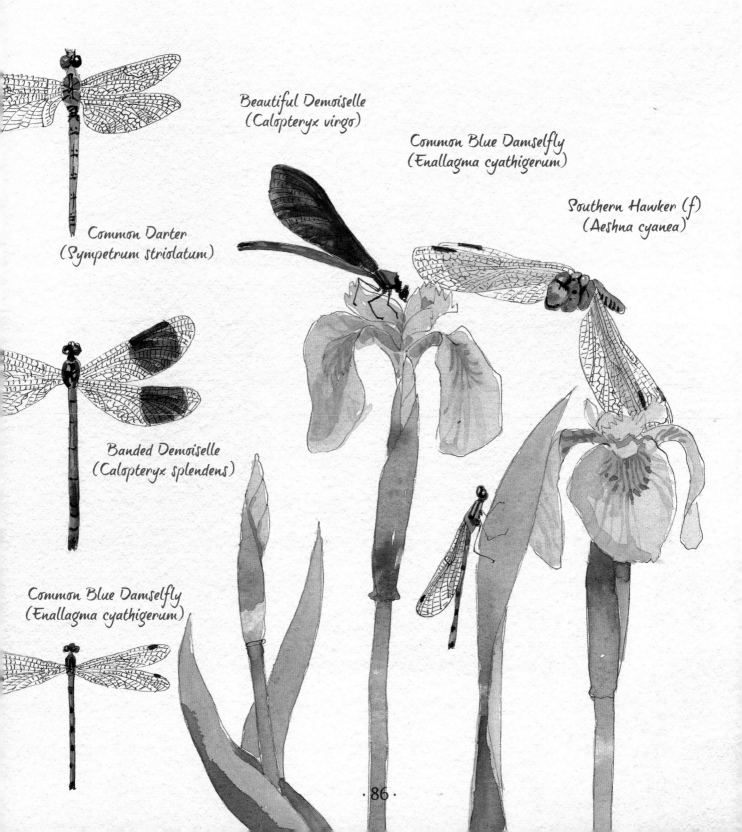

Beautiful Demoiselle
(Calopteryx virgo)

Common Blue Damselfly
(Enallagma cyathigerum)

Southern Hawker (f)
(Aeshna cyanea)

Common Darter
(Sympetrum striolatum)

Banded Demoiselle
(Calopteryx splendens)

Common Blue Damselfly
(Enallagma cyathigerum)

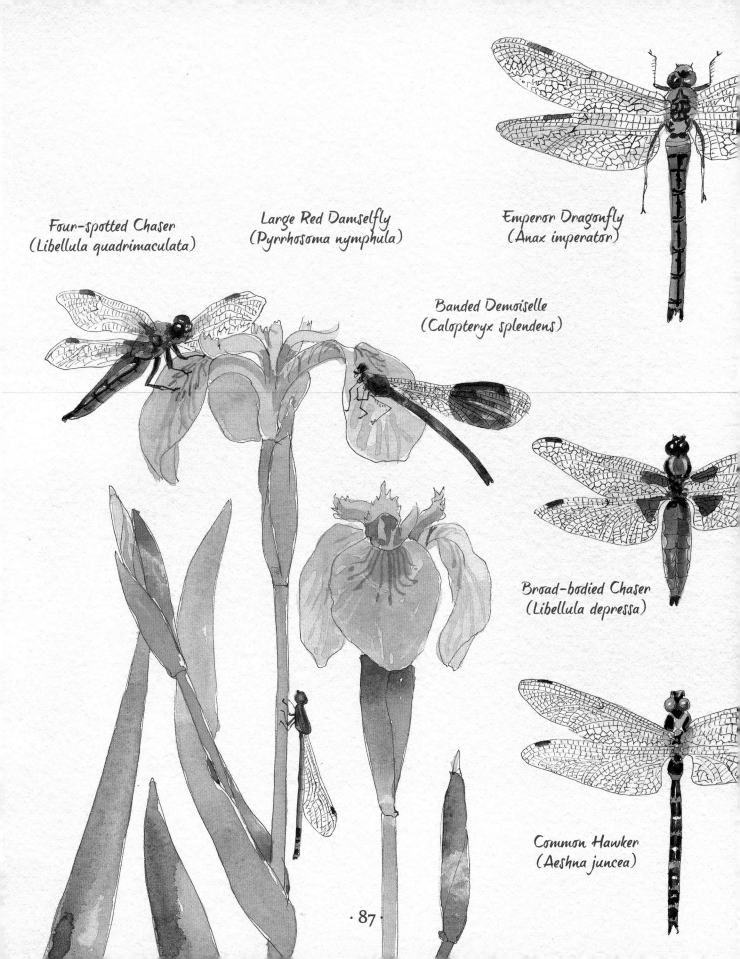

Four-spotted Chaser
(Libellula quadrimaculata)

Large Red Damselfly
(Pyrrhosoma nymphula)

Emperor Dragonfly
(Anax imperator)

Banded Demoiselle
(Calopteryx splendens)

Broad-bodied Chaser
(Libellula depressa)

Common Hawker
(Aeshna juncea)

Various grasses

1. Marsh Foxtail (*Alopecurus geniculatis*)

2. Meadow Foxtail (*Alopecurus pratensis*)

3. *Cynodon dactylon*

4. Common Bent Grass (*Agrostis capillaris*)

5. Common Wild Oat (*Avena fatua*)

6. Awnless Sheep's Fescue (*Festuca tenuifolia*)

7. Rye Grass (*Lolium perenne*)

8. Squirrel Tail (*Lordeum marinum*)

9. Meadow Fescue (*Festuca pratensis*)

10. Creeping Twitch (couch) (*Agropyron repens*)

11. Woodland Meadow Grass (*Poa nemoralis*)

12. Timothy Grass (*Phleum pretense*)

13 14 15   16   17 18 19   20   21 22 23

13. Wood Melick (*Melica uniflora*)

14. Common Quaking Grass (*Briza media*)

15. Wild Barley (*Hordeum murinum*)

16. Meadow Brome (*Bromus commutatus*)

17. Soft Brome (*Bromus mollis*)

18. Sheep's Fescue (*Festuca ovina*)

19. Purple Moor Grass (*Molinia cerulean*)

20. Reed Canary Grass (*Phalaris arundinacea*)

21. Velvet Bent (*Agrostis canina*)

22. Wood Millet (*Milium effusum*)

23. Lesser Cat's-tail (*Phleum bertolonii*)

June

Glow worms

There is something absolutely magical, almost unbelievable, about finding a glow worm, its glow is so astonishingly bright. Step out on a warm summer's evening and have a look around – you could be anywhere in the country but glow worms prefer open grassland or hedges to woodland. If you are lucky enough to spot one don't pick it up, these are rare creatures and must be left alone. Amazingly they are not the only creatures to emit luminescence – certain caterpillars and centipedes and even fungi also have this power, but none can match the brightness of the humble glow worm.

- Only female glow worms glow to attract males.

- The glow worm is not a worm but a beetle, reaching up to 25mm long.

- Adults do not feed and only live for around 14 days.

- Once she has mated the female turns off her light, lays her eggs and dies.

- The female has no wings.

- The eggs hatch into larvae and remain in a larval state for up to 3 years, feeding on small snails that they paralyse before sucking dry.

- June is the peak glowing season.

- Larvae also glow faintly and intermittently.

- The glow is a form of bioluminescence.

We are all worms but I do believe that I am a glow worm.

Winston Churchill

Wayside and woodland plants

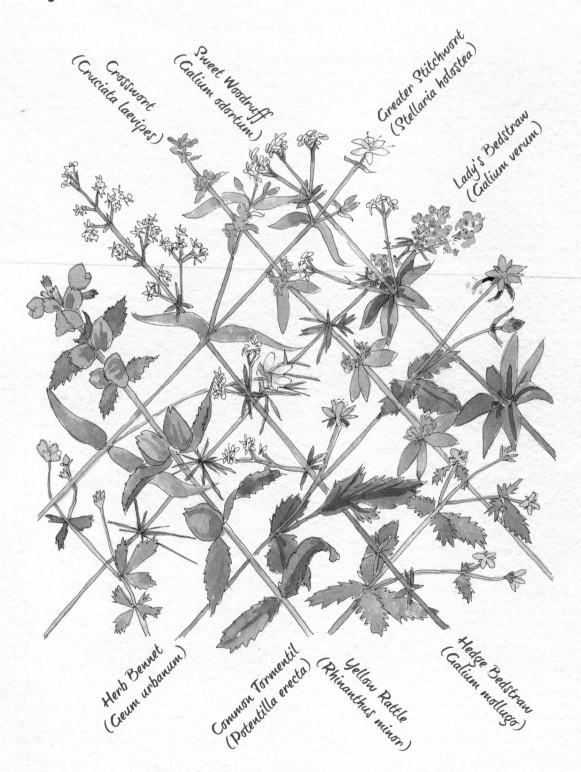

Crosswort
(Cruciata laevipes)

Sweet Woodruff
(Galium odoratum)

Greater Stitchwort
(Stellaria holostea)

Lady's Bedstraw
(Galium verum)

Herb Bennet
(Geum urbanum)

Common Tormentil
(Potentilla erecta)

Yellow Rattle
(Rhinanthus minor)

Hedge Bedstraw
(Galium mollugo)

June

Hawk-moths

Lime Hawk-moth (*Mimas tiliae*)

Found throughout Europe except in Scotland. The caterpillar feeds mainly on lime but also on elm, alder, birch and oak. When full grown it pupates underground. Commonly found flying in late spring to early summer.

Privet Hawk-moth (*Sphinx ligustri*)

Although common in Western Europe this moth has dropped in numbers in the UK. The caterpillars feed on privet, lilac and ash and when fully grown burrow deep into the ground to pupate.

Elephant Hawk-moth (*Deilephila elpenor*)

Common especially near willowherb, as this is the larval food plant. The caterpillars pupate on the ground in a silken cocoon strengthened with earth and bits of leaf.

Eyed Hawk-moth (*Smerinthus ocellata*)

Also found all over Europe, there is no doubting the derivation of this moth's name as it has distinct eyes on the underwings. These are hidden from view when the moth is at rest but if disturbed are suddenly revealed in order to scare any predator away.

Mullein Moth

The Mullein Moth (*Cucillia verbasci*) is so called because it particularly enjoys the leaves of the mullein (*Verbascum pulverulentum*), and can totally strip this large plant, although it also feeds on buddleia and figwort. Eggs are laid singly on the underneath of leaves.

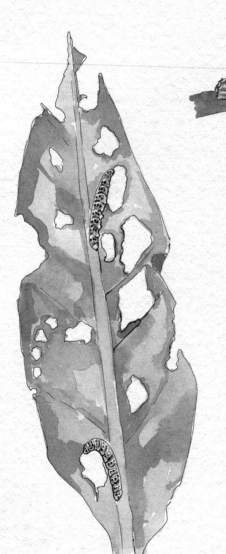

The caterpillars are most active between late May and mid-July and when ready to pupate wriggle down into the earth and spin a silk cocoon in which they chrysalise. They can spend up to 4 years in this state before hatching. Adult moths are very rarely seen as they are nocturnal and when stationary are well camouflaged.

June

Is it a bush cricket or grasshopper?

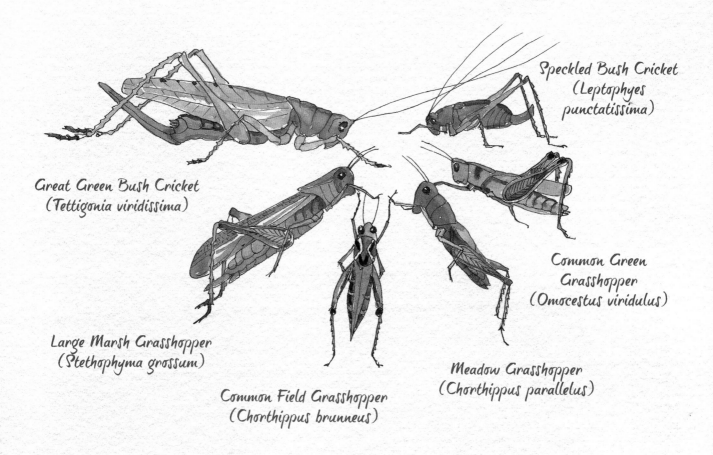

Speckled Bush Cricket
(Leptophyes
punctatissima)

Great Green Bush Cricket
(Tettigonia viridissima)

Common Green
Grasshopper
(Omocestus viridulus)

Large Marsh Grasshopper
(Stethophyma grossum)

Meadow Grasshopper
(Chorthippus parallelus)

Common Field Grasshopper
(Chorthippus brunneus)

Bush crickets and grasshoppers both belong to the order *Orthoptera*, but there are differences between them.

Crickets have long antennae whereas grasshoppers have short ones. Crickets sing or 'stridulate' by rubbing their wings together. Grasshoppers sing by rubbing their hind legs against their wings.

Both have 'ears' for detecting sounds, but crickets have them on their front legs while grasshoppers have them at the base of their abdomen.

Crickets are crepuscular (active during twilight hours) but grasshoppers are out and about during the day. Grasshoppers are vegetarian but crickets eat both grass and animal matter.

All except the Meadow Grasshopper can fly but as a rule move by hopping using their very long back legs to make long jumps. The larger females lay batches of eggs in pods that overwinter and hatch in the spring.

How to make a wildflower press

Never pick rare or endangered wildflowers – some species are protected and it is therefore an offence to do so. But there are plenty of common ones and you will soon discover which press best – fleshy ones, for instance, will take longer to press and some with white petals will dry brown. Experiment!

YOU WILL NEED:

  2 × 30 cm squares of MDF or plywood

  4 × 10 cm bolts + four wingnuts and washers

  4 × 30 cm square of cardboard with 3cm cut off the corners

  6 × 30 cm pieces of blotting paper with its corners cut off as well

Place one board exactly on top of the other and mark 2 cm in from the corners with a pencil dot. Drill a hole in each corner using a bit slightly larger than your bolt. Do them together to make sure the holes are directly on top of each other.

Make a sandwich: board, cardboard, blotting paper, blotting paper, cardboard, etc. until all is used up, insert the bolts and do up the wingnuts.

When placing your flowers in the press don't overlap them – lay them carefully, opening flower heads out and making sure leaves are not folded. Be patient – it will take around 2 weeks for your flowers to dry out and remain as they are.

They can be used on greeting cards, for pictures or be stuck in an album – your own wildflower collection.

Shorebirds

Avocet
(Recurvirostra avosetta)

Curlew
(Numenius arquata)

Common Sandpiper
(Actitis hypoleucos)

Dunlin
(Calidris alpina)

Greenshank
(Tringa nebularia)

Oystercatcher
(Haematopus ostralegus)

Turnstone
(Arenaria interpres)

June

Painted Lady

The Painted Lady (*Vanessa cardui*) is possibly the most widespread butterfly in the world, occurring in North and South America, Europe, Asia and Africa.

- This butterfly is a migrant visitor to the UK, sometimes arriving in hundreds of thousands from northern Africa, returning there in the autumn.

- The largest migration recorded worldwide numbered a possible 300 million.

- When migrating they fly low over the ground, between 2 and 3m high.

- They can cover up to 100 miles in a day and can fly at up to 30 miles per hour.

- Caterpillars love thistles – in fact *Vanessa cardui* means 'butterfly of thistles' and is perhaps how this particular insect has spread so far, as thistles grow in most regions of the world.

- Male Painted Ladies are territorial, chasing competing males away while waiting patiently for a female. Mating takes place at night.

- When the caterpillars hatch they form a silken nest over themselves as protection from predators, which include birds, dragonflies and other insect eaters.

- This species of butterfly cannot survive European winters and must return to Africa or die.

*Spear Thistle
(Cirsium vulgare)*

*Marsh Thistle
(Cirsium palustre)*

Otters

The European Otter (*Lutra lutra*) belongs to the family Mustelidae, which includes badgers, weasels, stoats and pine martens. Otters live by water and are as happy with seawater as they are with lakes and rivers. Males (dogs) and females (bitches) reach breeding age at two years and although there is no specific breeding season, spring is the most likely time for them to produce a litter, depending on the availability of food. Mating takes place in the water and each litter consists of one or two cubs that are born blind in a burrow known as a holt, and are totally helpless for their first six weeks. They stay with their mother for up to 18 months.

An otter's staple diet is fish, in particular eels and crustaceans, but being carnivores they will eat anything they can catch including birds and small mammals.

Very agile swimmers, otters can slow their heart rate to reduce oxygen consumption under water. Their long whiskers are so sensitive that they can detect the approach of a fish.

They have no predators apart from humans, but loss of habitat also means that this charming animal is rare. In the 1950s and 60s otters almost died out in the UK as a result of organochlorine pesticides and pollution, but numbers are beginning to increase, boosted by reintroduction programmes.

Otters have small ears, round eyes and flattish heads; their ears and nostrils can close when under water and webbed feet ensure that they are strong swimmers. Although naturally shy, they are unmistakable when moving on land, with their lolloping gait, and once in the water they swim close to the surface with just their head and back showing until they dive, when the whole tail is visible looping over as they disappear.

June

Scallops with samphire

Samphire grows in muddy estuaries and salt marshes and appears from June onwards. Snap off the upper branches and rinse thoroughly in clean water. Samphire with scallops is a marriage made in heaven and takes less than 5 minutes to prepare. Samphire is also delicious on its own or with any fish.

You might be lucky enough to find your own scallops but these are shellfish that remain below the low water mark – you will either have to dive or wade about on the lowest of low spring tides. Today most of the scallops in fishmongers are farmed.

YOU WILL NEED:

large bunch of samphire

2 scallops per person
(or more if you're feeling generous!)

1 lemon

butter to fry the scallops

Place the samphire in a saucepan of boiling water – it takes only a minute or two to cook. Meanwhile fry the scallops in a frying pan or better still a griddle, for one minute on each side. Share out the samphire on to individual plates and pop the scallops on top. Squeeze some lemon juice over – what more could you want!

Beech

TYPE *Fagus sylvatica* is a broadleaf deciduous tree, belonging to the same family as the olive tree.

SIZE Up to 40 m.

BARK Pale grey with fine pattern of criss-crossing ridges. Once used to treat malaria as a substitute for cinchona bark, which was used to make quinine.

FOLIAGE Buds appear black. Produces small coral-coloured flowers. The leaf has six to twelve pairs of thin oval (pinnate) leaflets with a long stalk. Often the last tree to come into leaf in May. Loses its leaves, often all in one go, after the first frost.

FRUIT Winged keys in clusters that turn brown after leaf fall.

USES Once used by Anglo Saxons for spears and shield handles as the wood is strong and flexible and is still used for such diverse things as oars, gates, wheel rims, tools and walking sticks.

June

July

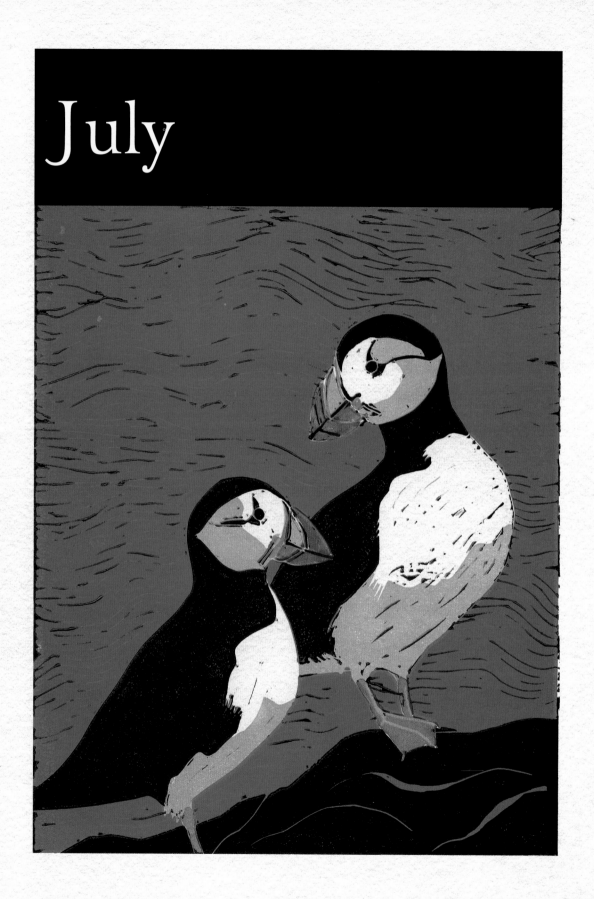

This saying has some sense in it, as if the weather hasn't settled into balmy days by this time of year then it probably won't, but if it is fine and dry then we're likely to have at least a month of good weather. Hot weather can also bring thunderstorms, but heavy short showers rather than prolonged rain usually accompany these.

The flowers of trees and shrubs will be over and the fruit will be swelling, and there is a general feeling of heaviness about the woods. It's a good month for beachcombing and seeing how many different shells and objects you can find.

Puffins are one of our most delightful birds, often called the clowns of the sea. They spend most of their lives at sea, just coming ashore to breed. They excavate burrows in turf on cliff tops, sometimes using ones left by rabbits or even managing to eject the rabbit itself. The female lays a single egg, and the parents work very hard to feed the chick with sandeels, which they cleverly manage to carry head to tail in their strange bill, thanks to its serrated edges. The chick soon gets very fat on this nourishing food – in fact it reaches a point where it is too large to leave the burrow! The parents then abandon it and it has to wait until it has slimmed down to emerge from the burrow and leap bravely from the cliff. Puffins actually 'fly' under water using their feet as rudders.

July

Cinnabar Moth and Ragwort

The **Cinnabar Moth** (*Tyria jacobaeae*) is a day-flying moth, its brightly coloured wings warning birds that it is unpalatable. The larvae feed exclusively on the genus Senecio and in particular Ragwort. Eggs are laid in large batches of up to 300 eggs and the brightly coloured black and yellow larvae absorb the toxic and bitter substances of their food plants, thereby rendering themselves inedible.

If there is a shortage of food the larvae can turn cannibalistic and the fact that so many eggs are laid in one place often causes the food source to be reduced, resulting in death from starvation.

Common Ragwort (*Senecio jacobaea*) is a common native biennial (not to be confused with Oxford Ragwort, which is a foreign coloniser) that quickly colonises waste ground and supports an astonishing 77 invertebrate species, of which 30 are entirely dependent on it. It is also an important nectar source for butterflies, moths and bees. The Code of Practice for implementing the Ragwort Control Act 2004 states that it 'does not propose the eradication of common ragwort but promotes a strategic approach to control the spread of common ragwort where it poses a threat to the health and welfare of grazing animals and the production of feed or forage'.

Gorse

Gorse (*Ulex europaeus*) is a prickly bush found all over the country, especially on sunny, acid, dry soils. Gorse is also known as furze or whin and has a surprising number of uses.

- It has a pea-like flower with a coconut scent.

- Gorse is an important nesting site for, in particular, Dartford Warbler, Stonechat and Whinchat.

- It is the food plant of, among others, the Double-striped Pug Moth, Green Hairstreak and Silver-studded Blue larvae.

- When bruised with a wooden mallet it is used as a traditional cattle fodder.

- Gorse is often used as a windbreak.

- It is highly flammable and was once used to fire bread ovens, though Gorse seeds can survive flames.

- Gorse pods burst open in July.

- Three species of gorse are found in Britain: Common, Western and Dwarf Gorse.

- Its flowers are found all year round but mainly in spring (hence the saying below).

- Gorse flowers are edible and can be added to salad and made into wine or cordial.

Stonechat

When gorse is in flower kissing is in season.

July

Earthworms

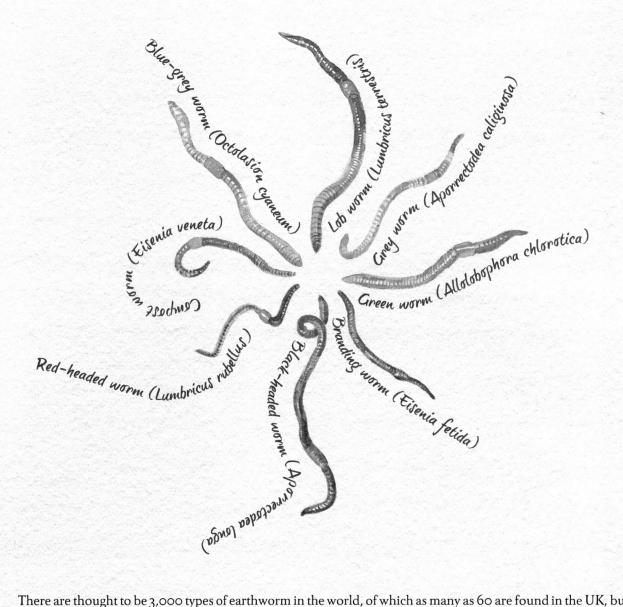

Blue-grey worm (Octolasion cyaneum)

Lob worm (Lumbricus terrestris)

Grey worm (Aporrectodea caliginosa)

Green worm (Allolobophora chlorotica)

Compost worm (Eisenia veneta)

Branding worm (Eisenia fetida)

Red-headed worm (Lumbricus rubellus)

Black-headed worm (Aporrectodea longa)

There are thought to be 3,000 types of earthworm in the world, of which as many as 60 are found in the UK, but of those only 26 are indigenous, the others being exotic introductions found in glasshouses, etc.

A worm is basically a digestive tube divided into segments, the mouth being in the first segment. They are hermaphrodites and when ready to mate adopt a head-to-tail position, cover themselves with mucus and exchange sperm. The worm casts that you see on the soil are simply faeces. Worms have an important role to play in the breakdown of organic matter, thereby releasing nutrients back into the soil.

Butterflies and nettles

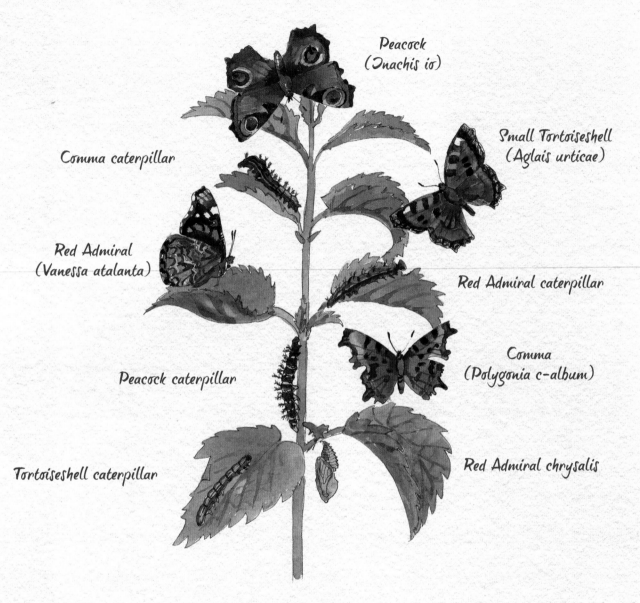

Peacock
(Inachis io)

Small Tortoiseshell
(Aglais urticae)

Comma caterpillar

Red Admiral
(Vanessa atalanta)

Red Admiral caterpillar

Peacock caterpillar

Comma
(Polygonia c-album)

Tortoiseshell caterpillar

Red Admiral chrysalis

Stinging nettles (*Urtica dioica*) are an important food plant in the butterfly world, in fact the **Red Admiral**, **Tortoiseshell** and **Peacock** larvae feed on nothing else. Peacocks and Tortoiseshells lay their eggs in batches on the undersides of the leaves and when the caterpillars hatch they weave themselves a silken tent to live under. The Red Admiral lays single eggs on the top of the leaves and the caterpillar wraps itself in a leaf when it hatches with silken strands. The **Comma**, although favouring nettles, also lays its eggs on a variety of plants. The eggs are laid on the top of a leaf but immediately it hatches the larvae crawls underneath and perforates the leaf from this safer position.

July

Picked up on a sandy shore

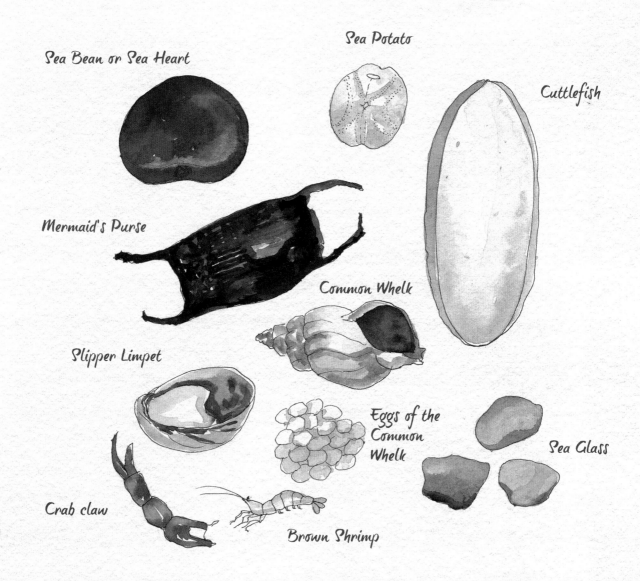

Sea Bean or Sea Heart

Sea Potato

Cuttlefish

Mermaid's Purse

Common Whelk

Slipper Limpet

Eggs of the Common Whelk

Sea Glass

Crab claw

Brown Shrimp

Sea Bean or Sea Heart: It was one of these that supposedly led Columbus to realise there must be new land to the west, as they do not come from any European plant. They are in fact the fruit of the Monkey Vine of South America and float across the Atlantic on the Gulf Stream.

Mermaid's Purse: the egg case of skate, dogfish, sharks or rays.

Sea Potato: the shell of the Heart Urchin.

Cuttlefish Bone or Cuttlebone: the hard internal shell found in all members of the cuttlefish family to help control buoyancy.

Sea Glass: glass that has been weathered by rolling in sand at the bottom of the sea and that as a result has rounded edges.

Seals

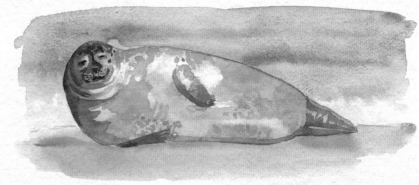

Common Seals (*Phoca vitulina*), also
known as Harbour Seals, are found all
over the North Atlantic and North Pacific Oceans and are extremely common, in fact they are the most widespread
of the pinnipeds (mammals that have finlike flippers for locomotion). About 5% of the total population of Common
Seals live around the British Isles. A female can live as long as 30 years but males seldom survive beyond 20. They
eat a wide variety of fish and crustaceans, tearing their prey to bits and swallowing it without chewing.

Seals can be seen lying on rocky shores or sandbanks, where they haul themselves out to rest, sometimes
resembling giant bananas. They also give birth ashore, often returning to the same place year after year. Females
give birth to a single pup in June or July; the pups are very well developed at birth, capable of swimming at just a few
hours old. A seal's milk is particularly rich and pups double
their birth weight in three to four weeks. Common
Seals moult annually, generally shortly after
breeding and during this time spend a good
deal of their time ashore.

Atlantic Grey Seal (*Halichoerus grypus*)
is the larger of the two seal species and
there is a marked difference in size between
the sexes – the males can reach 2.5 m and weigh
350 kg, whereas the smaller females are 2 m long and
weigh 200 kg. Pups are born at traditional pupping sites known
as rookeries, with a white fluffy coat known as 'lanugo', meaning not waterproof, as a result of which they must
spend their first few weeks ashore while suckling. The pups then moult and gain their adult waterproof coats.

Atlantic Grey Seals have a similar diet to Common Seals and can dive to a depth of up to 200 m. Almost half the
world population of Atlantic Greys live around the British Isles.

July

Gulls

Common Gull (*Larus canus*): resembling a smaller and more elegant version of the Herring Gull, regardless of its name this gull is not particularly common. Nests are simple affairs of vegetation or seaweed formed on the ground and usually in colonies near water, particularly coastal marshes.

Common Gull

Herring Gull

Herring Gull (*Larus argentatus*): vary in size from almost as small as a Common Gull to almost as large as a Great Black-backed Gull. They can be distinguished from Kittiwakes by their pink legs and from Great Black-backed Gulls by their much paler mantle (or saddleback). This is a very common gull that can often be seen perched on a favourite telegraph pole or mast.

Great Black-backed Gull
(*Larus marinus*): the largest of
our gulls, very similar, though
darker and larger than the Lesser
Black-backed Gull. These and
the Herring Gull are easy to
confuse at different stages of their
adolescence and can only really be
told apart when fully grown and
in breeding plumage.

Great Black-backed Gull

Kittiwake (*Rissa tridactyla*): this is a pretty little gull that loves high sea cliffs and
even nests on cliff ledges in breeding colonies when the cry of 'kitt-ee-wayke'
can be easily distinguished. The nest is made of mud, seaweed and grass and is
much sturdier than the average
gull, perhaps fortunately
as this prevents the eggs
rolling off the edge. After
breeding they move
out into the Atlantic to
spend the winter often
accompanying whales or
other sea mammals on
their travels.

Kittiwake

July

Is it a Red-legged or Grey Partridge?

Red-legged Partridge

Both these species are gallinaceous gamebirds of the pheasant family. They both spend much of their life on the ground and run rather than fly, although they can fly short distances gliding on rounded wings. They are rarely seen in trees. They are seed eaters although the young of both species also eat insects. Both group together in flocks of up to 20 birds known as coveys. Pairs mate for life (although bigamy is not unknown). When they hatch the chicks are precocial (covered in down on hatching and immediately active).

The **Red-legged or French Partridge** (*Alectoris rufa*) is slightly larger than the Grey Partridge. Its head has a white stripe above a red eye and beak, white chin and black collar. The body has obvious black, chestnut and white bars, with a grey-blue breast and marked red legs.

Nesting takes place on the ground in bushy scrub or hedges. Sometimes females lay a second clutch in a separate nest, in which case the male and female brood one each – an unusual breeding system known as double-clutching.

Grey Partridge

The **Grey or English Partridge** (*Perdix perdix*) has a brown-black and grey streaked back and chest, pale breast with a large dark brown horseshoe mark and orange face, making them well camouflaged in long grass. Generally they lay up to 20 eggs in a nest on the ground at the margin of a cereal field. Unlike the Red-legged Partridge they carefully cover their eggs with grass or leaves when they are absent.

July

How to make a shell mobile

Half the fun of making a shell mobile is hunting for the shells themselves. Perhaps they have memories of holidays – or the whole family can contribute as it doesn't matter which shells are used or if they are perfect specimens. If you can't find a suitable bit of driftwood any branch will do or you could use a circle of wire designed for a wreath that can be bought at florists.

YOU WILL NEED:

   A piece of driftwood

   A quantity of different shells – broken ones are fine

   A length of fishing cast or cotton

For a neat finish drill small holes in your piece of driftwood and attach a length of cast. Tie your shells at intervals – you'll be able to thread the cast easily through broken shells but perfect ones will need to have a small hole drilled through them.

White Admiral and Honeysuckle

The **White Admiral** (*Limenitis camilla*) loves woodland glades and will usually be found where honeysuckle grows, as this is the larval food plant. Males and females are similar in appearance although the female is very slightly larger. Wings are black and white on top but the undersides are beautifully marked in chestnut and white. The adults sip honeydew, particularly favouring bramble flowers. Single eggs are laid on shady patches of honeysuckle and when the light brown larva emerges it eats the shell before moving to the leaf tip to feed.

In the autumn the larva builds a hibernaculum, or winter shelter, by securing the leaf to a twig with silk (to make sure the leaf stays attached when others fall) and then folding the edges together. When the larva emerges in the spring it moults again and turns a bright green. The pupa is formed under a leaf or stem and the adult butterfly emerges in 2 to 3 weeks.

Honeysuckle (*Lonicera periclymenum*) is also known as woodbine. Suck the end of a Honeysuckle flower and you'll discover why it is so named. The sweet scent is particularly strong at night and attracts moths to its trumpet-shaped flowers.

According to an old superstition, if Honeysuckle is taken into a house then a wedding will follow. If a girl places this fragrant flower in her bedroom, she will dream of love, and in France it was given to a loved one to symbolise their union.

July

Bats

There is only one mammal capable of true flight and that is the bat. Astonishingly there are over 1,000 species of bat in the world and 45 species in Europe, of which 18 are found in the UK.

Bats are insectivores and each species has its own favourite prey. Flying uses a lot of energy and insects are not very energy giving so bats have to work very hard to maintain themselves, eating up to 3,000 small insects in a single night. Bats have very small eyes but their ears are more important as they find their way around and locate their prey using echolocation. They are so expert at reading the information received that they can tell which way an insect is going and its size.

Bats spend the day in roosts – these may be hollow trees, caves or house roofs and hanging tiles. Mating takes place in late autumn and the female stores the sperm, not becoming pregnant until the spring. Pregnant females gather into maternity roosts and generally have one baby, which they suckle for 4 or 5 weeks.

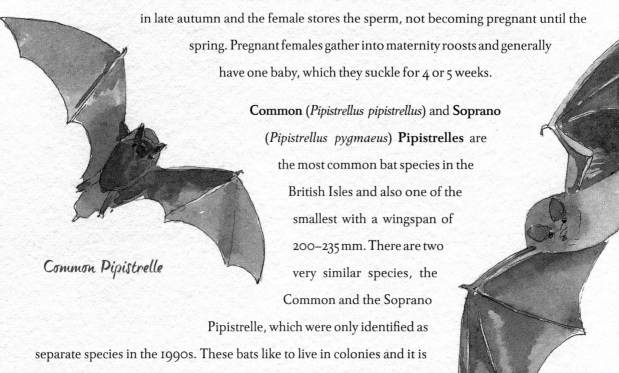

Common Pipistrelle

Daubenton's Bat

Common (*Pipistrellus pipistrellus*) and **Soprano** (*Pipistrellus pygmaeus*) **Pipistrelles** are the most common bat species in the British Isles and also one of the smallest with a wingspan of 200–235 mm. There are two very similar species, the Common and the Soprano Pipistrelle, which were only identified as separate species in the 1990s. These bats like to live in colonies and it is not unusual to find maternity roosts of up to 1,000 bats.

Daubenton's Bat (*Myotis daubentonii*) is a medium-sized bat (wingspan 240–275 mm) that feeds by flying low over slow-moving or still water and can pick insects off the water surface with its feet. They can swim and are able to take off from the surface of the water. Tunnels and bridges or caves are their favoured roosts and colonies average 20 to 50 bats, although up to 200 have been recorded.

Greater Horseshoe Bat (*Rhinolophus ferrumequinum*) is one of the UK's largest bats (wingspan 330–400 mm), with a horseshoe-shaped nose used as part of its echolocation system, these bats are now becoming more of a rarity. The bats emerge from their roosts within half an hour of sunset and catch insects in flight and on the ground but occasionally behave like flycatchers, finding a perch and flying out to take passing prey.

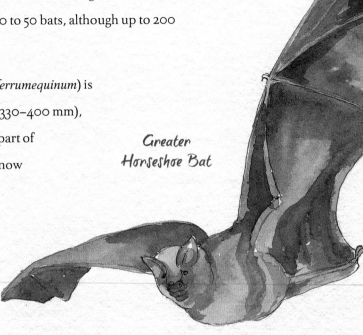

Greater
Horseshoe Bat

Once cave dwellers, the bats are now more likely to breed in buildings with large entrance holes such as churches and barns. Maternity colonies can be noisy with constant chattering and chirping. These bats can live for an amazing 30 years and the females do not become sexually mature until their third year – they may not breed every year.

Brown Long-eared Bat (*Plecotus auritus*) is a medium-sized bat with a 230–285 mm wingspan with huge ears that are nearly as long as the creature's body. The bats are capable of curling their ears back like rams' horns or tucking them under their wings so they are not always obvious. These bats are sometimes known as 'whispering bats' as their echolocation sounds are very quiet. They fly slowly amongst foliage, picking insects off leaves and bark and occasionally catching them on the ground. Large insects are taken to a regular perch to be consumed, the signs of which can be accumulations of moth wings or insect remains on the floor.

Brown Long-eared Bat

July

RECITE

Rosehip syrup

Rosa canina, the wild dog rose that flowers in hedgerows in early summer, produces the lovely shiny scarlet hips in late summer. These are a natural source of vitamin C and bioflavanoids. Rosehips have all kinds of herbal uses, including easing of joints in a way similar to, though apparently better than, glucosamine. They also prevent urinary tract infections and ease headaches. During the Second World War rosehips became such an important source of vitamins that children were paid 3d per pound to harvest them.

The syrup will keep for a few weeks in the fridge – freeze any excess in plastic bottles until needed.

YOU WILL NEED:

1 kg rosehips

2 litres boiling water

500 g sugar

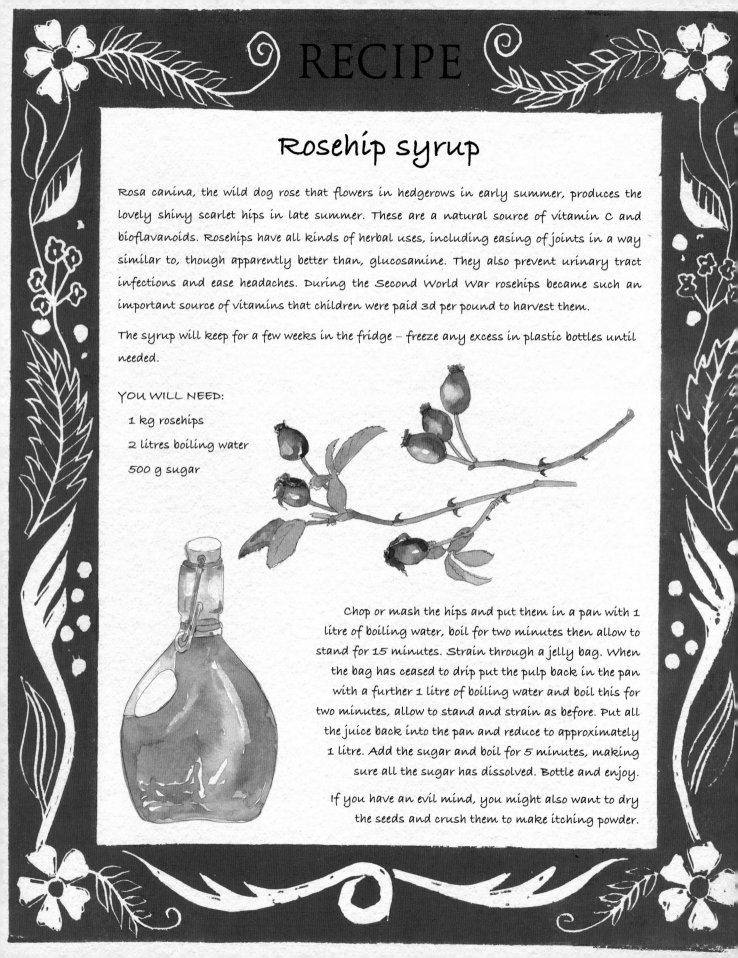

Chop or mash the hips and put them in a pan with 1 litre of boiling water, boil for two minutes then allow to stand for 15 minutes. Strain through a jelly bag. When the bag has ceased to drip put the pulp back in the pan with a further 1 litre of boiling water and boil this for two minutes, allow to stand and strain as before. Put all the juice back into the pan and reduce to approximately 1 litre. Add the sugar and boil for 5 minutes, making sure all the sugar has dissolved. Bottle and enjoy.

If you have an evil mind, you might also want to dry the seeds and crush them to make itching powder.

Sycamore

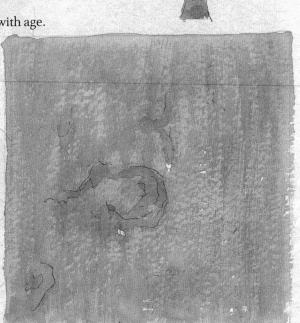

TYPE *Acer pseudoplatanus* is a very common deciduous broadleaf tree, found in all locations in Europe and was probably introduced to the UK by the Romans.

SIZE 16–35 m.

BARK Pinky-grey and smooth, becoming slightly rougher with age.

FOLIAGE Five lobed palmate leaves with long red stalks.

FLOWERS AND SEEDS Yellowish tails of tiny flowers in April. Bunches of large winged keys, tinged red but turning rust-coloured when ripe, which spiral to the ground and carried by the wind can land some distance from the parent tree. The seeds germinate abundantly.

USES As this tree copes well with pollution it is often found in cities and city parks as a shade tree. The timber is as strong as oak but not as long-lived, but is commonly used to make kitchen tables and domestic utensils such as rolling pins. Sycamores are straight grained but the occasional tree develops a beautiful wavy grain which is known as 'fiddleback' and is used to make the backs of violins.

July

August

When the dew is in the grass
Rain will never come to pass.
When grass is dry at morning light,
Look for rain before the night.

The trees are heavy with foliage and the grass is beginning to die but some flowers are only just starting to come out and heather is one of them. Beloved of bees, a stretch of heather moorland or heath actually smells of honey on a sunny day.

Blackberries, one of our most versatile foraging foods, will be ripening and there will be plenty of food around for wild mammals, birds and insects. Hazelnuts won't yet be ripe but the squirrels will be feasting on them none the less.

Take a walk on a beach and see what you can find – all sorts of fascinating things are there, you just need to look and think what unusual use they can be put to.

August

Common wildflowers

Bindweed: a perennial that twines round other plants in an anti-clockwise direction with broad (3–7 cm) trumpet-shaped flowers.

Comfrey: also known as knitbone, from when it was a herbal remedy to heal torn ligaments and broken bones. The leaves can be used as a mulch in the garden because they are high in nitrogen, phosphorus and potash.

Horehound: a perennial herb found all over Europe with a strong smell. Once used to treat an upset stomach and travel sickness but never very popular thanks to its foul odour.

Yellow Pimpernel: a very common wildflower rather similar to Creeping Jenny with star-shaped bright yellow flowers. It is a lover of shady damp places.

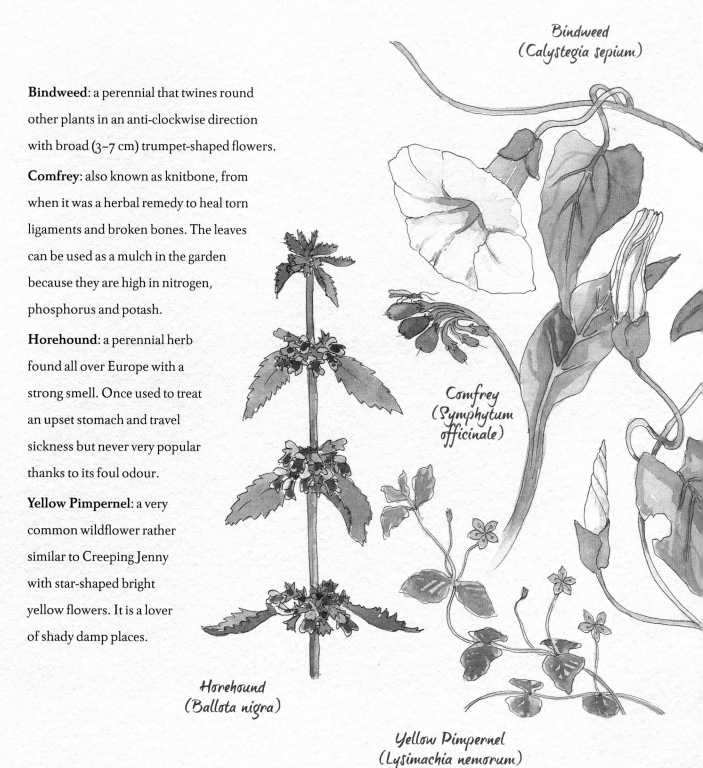

Bindweed
(Calystegia sepium)

Comfrey
(Symphytum officinale)

Horehound
(Ballota nigra)

Yellow Pimpernel
(Lysimachia nemorum)

Robin's Pincushion

The grubs inside the gall feed on the host through winter and emerge in spring as adults. Robin's Pincushion (also known as the Bedeguar Gall) is commonly found on Dog Rose (Rosa canina) and is caused by the larvae of the tiny gall wasp (Diploepsis rosae).

August

How to make a driftwood lamp

Half the fun of making a driftwood lamp is hunting for the driftwood itself. Some beaches have a dearth of wood so you will have to find one where the tide washes it ashore. Driftwood comes ready sanded by the sea but when you get it home give it a rinse and soak it in a plastic bowl of water with bleach added to give it a lovely clean look and also to be sure there is nothing living in it.

You might choose a few large pieces, lots of small ones or a mixture. You can twist them round the stem or have them all facing one way in a vertical row, the choice is yours.

YOU WILL NEED:

    A lamp with a tall narrow stem

    Drill with smallest drill bit

    Roll of florist's wire

Drill a hole in the middle of each bit of driftwood, thread a small amount of wire through and attach it neatly to your lamp. As long as the pieces sit nicely together the wire will be invisible – what could be simpler?

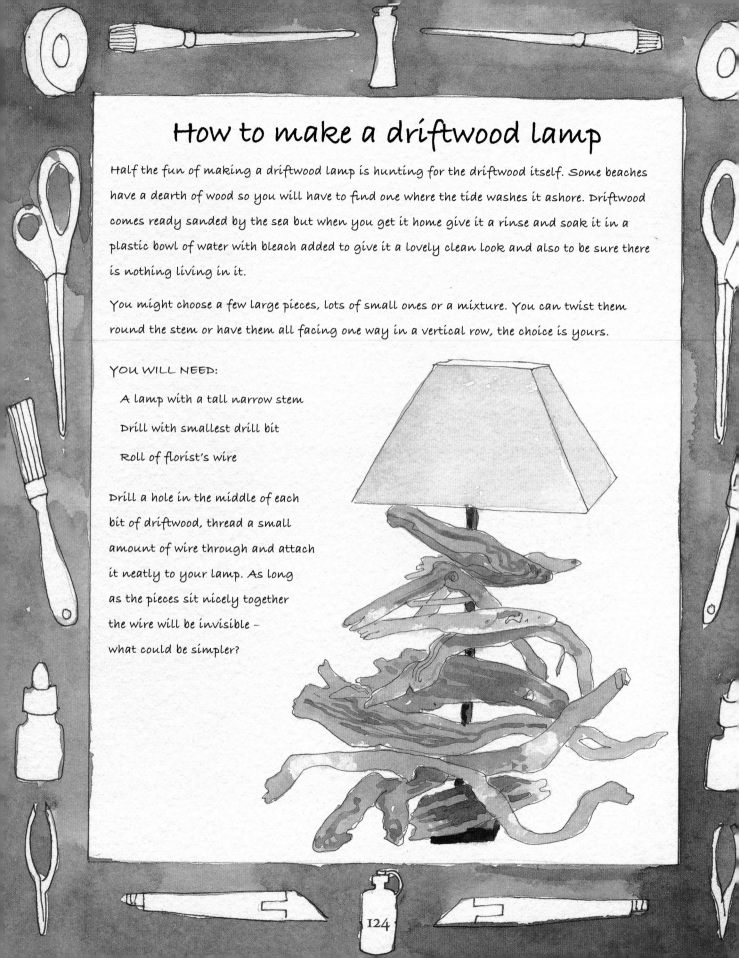

Picked up on a west coast shore

All sorts of fascinating things float onto a rocky shore, one of the most amazing of which is the urchin shell. Its prickles all having fallen out, it becomes so light it simply drifts gently onto the shore and sits there unbroken. There are several types of urchin in European waters – the pink one illustrated here is the Common or Edible Sea Urchin.

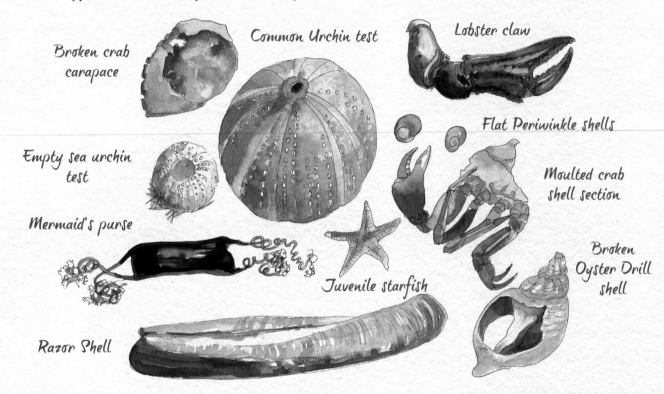

Broken crab carapace

Common Urchin test

Lobster claw

Flat Periwinkle shells

Empty sea urchin test

Moulted crab shell section

Mermaid's purse

Broken Oyster Drill shell

Juvenile starfish

Razor Shell

You can find crab shells and claws, perhaps even a lobster claw. Shells may be broken but that has the advantage of letting you look inside the whorl of the whelk. Razor Shells are also edible but hard to catch. If you want to try you must first spot the Razor Shell's burrow at low tide, and pour some salt into the hole. The clam will come up to the surface but you will have to be very quick indeed to dig it out as the shell can burrow at an astonishing rate.

The baby starfish was probably picked up by a bird and deposited on the beach when it discovered it wasn't good to eat, and nearly every beach will have the little yellow, brown or white periwinkles.

The small mermaid's purse with a mass of tendrils attached to each corner is the empty egg case of the Lesser Spotted Dogfish.

August

White flowers

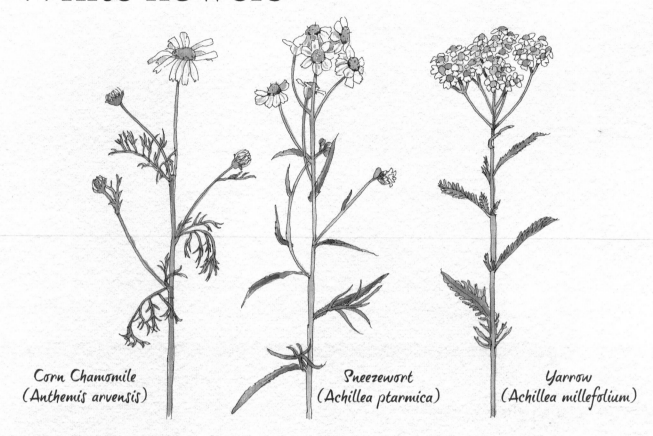

Corn Chamomile
(Anthemis arvensis)

Sneezewort
(Achillea ptarmica)

Yarrow
(Achillea millefolium)

Several species of Mayweed look similar but **Corn Chamomile** has slightly less feathery and hairy leaves. The leaves release scent when walked on and in the Middle Ages it was used as a strewing herb and grown in paths specifically to be walked over. English country folk have grown it for centuries as a domestic medicine.

Sneezewort is a native perennial common in damp meadows and marshes found all over Europe except the Mediterranean. The flowers appear from June until October. When dried and powdered it produces an effective sneezing powder or snuff although there is some dispute as to whether the leaves or the roots are most effective. The leaves can also be chewed to give relief from toothache and when crushed act as an insect repellent.

Yarrow or **Milfoil** is a common native flower that tolerates most soil types; the flowers may be pink on acid soil. It flowers from June to September. Long known as a topical healing herb to dress wounds, its scientific name originates because Achilles carried it with him into battle. In the middle ages yarrow was used to flavour beer prior to the use of hops. Another use, thanks to its bloodclotting capabilities, is to stem nosebleeds. Strangely this herb can be used not only to stop bleeding but, depending on how it is administered, to promote it.

August flowers

Giant Bellflower
(Campanula latifolia)

Rosebay Willowherb
(Epilobium augustifolium)

Meadow Cranesbill
(Geranium pratense)

Meadowsweet
(Filipendula ulmaria)

Betony
(Betonica officinalis)

Harebell
(Campanula rotundifolia)

August

Is it a hornet or a wasp?

There are many species of wasp in Europe, but the most common are the hornet and the common wasp.

Hornets (*Vespa crabro*) are the largest wasp found in the UK (35 mm) and differ from common wasps not only in size but also colour. The wasp is yellow and black whereas the hornet is yellow and brown.

They build similar nests to wasps, made of a papery material created by scraping wood from trees and mixing it with saliva. Usually they nest in holes in trees. Unlike wasps they fly at night and are attracted by light.

Although hornets are rather fearsome-looking creatures they are supposedly docile and will only sting if seriously provoked.

The **Common Wasp** (*Vespula vulgaris*) can sometimes be mistaken for a honey bee. Wasps have yellow legs and shiny sleek yellow and black bodies. Wasps are considerably more aggressive than hornets and build their nests in the ground or commonly in garden sheds, in a similar way to hornets. The queen builds the first small nest and tends the larvae herself. As soon as they hatch the worker wasps take over and enlarge the nest.

Spiders

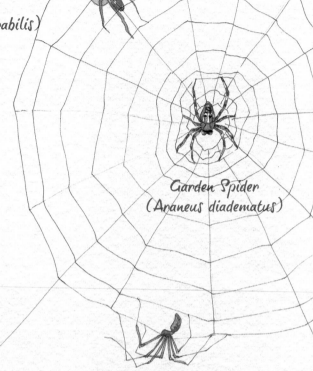

Nursery Web
Spider
(*Pisaura mirabilis*)

Garden Spider
(*Araneus diadematus*)

Daddy Long-legs Spider
(*Pholcus phalangioides*)

Spiders are found almost everywhere in the world, from the coldest place to the hottest.

- There are around 40,000 species of spider in the world, with around 600 in the UK.

- Spiders are not insects but arachnids.

- They differ from insects in that they have eight legs rather than six and two body parts rather than three.

- Spiders have eight simple eyes instead of two compound ones.

- They have no antennae but on the front of the spider's head are palps, which are similar to an insect's antennae and provide an important role in identification.

- Spiders never have wings.

- All of a spider's legs are attached to its head.

- The silk glands are housed in the abdomen and produce silk that may be sticky, smooth, rigid or stretchy.

- The silk is discharged by spinnerets at the tip of the abdomen.

- They are also used by the male to place sperm in the female's genital opening.

- All spiders are carnivorous.

- They inject deadly poison into their prey with their fangs and this contains digestive enzymes that liquidise their victim's insides, which they then drink, leaving an empty skin.

- Not all spiders use webs to catch their food – some jump on their prey.

- In order not to get caught in their own webs, spiders coat their legs with an oily substance from their mouths.

- Spider silk is twice as strong as steel and the strongest natural material known.

Zebra Spider
(*Salticus scenicus*)

August

House Spider
(*Tegenaria gigantean*)

Blackberry and raspberry vinegar

Blackberries must be the most versatile of food than can be picked for free and they make wonderful jellies, jams and puddings, but here is a slightly different use for them that makes an unusual salad dressing or – and this may sound strange – a sweet but slightly sharp sauce that can simply be poured on ice cream or anything else you fancy.

YOU WILL NEED:

500 g blackberries, washed

600–700 ml white wine vinegar

Sugar (quantity depends on how much juice you end up with)

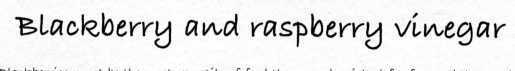

Pick your blackberries, wash them well and put them in a shallow dish.

Cover with the white wine vinegar and leave to steep, stirring occasionally, for between 3 and 5 days – the longer the better. Strain the blackberries through a jelly bag overnight.

Measure the juice into a saucepan and for every 500 ml add 300 g sugar.

Bring to the boil, stirring to dissolve the sugar.

Boil for 2 minutes then allow to cool a little before pouring into sterilised bottles. It will keep for several months.

Exactly the same can be made with wild raspberries – these little jewels of fruit are smaller than the commercially grown ones and take a lot of picking but are just as flavourful. Dilute with hot water to make a drink to relieve sore throats and flu symptoms.

Common Lime

TYPE *Tilia europa* is a naturally occurring hybrid between the Large-leaved Lime and the Small-leaved Lime and more common than both. Large deciduous tree common in towns that is tolerant to many conditions and soil types, also known as Linden.

SIZE 20–40 m

BARK Pale greyish-brown with irregular ridges. Twigs often shoot from burrs at the base of the trunk. The inner bark, known as 'bass', was once used in the making of mats and ropes

FOLIAGE Bright green leaves with paler undersides.

FLOWERS AND SEEDS Flowers are arranged in groups on a long stalk with a green leaf-like bract attached above. The round furry fruits are dispersed with the bract, which floats them away from the tree.

USES Makes good fuel and is also used by woodturners, in particular to make musical instruments. One more unusual use was for the sticks used by Morris dancers. Tea can be made by infusing the flowers in boiling water and this supposedly gives relief from coughs, colds and headaches.

August

September

If dry be the buck's horn' On Holyrood morn,

'Tis worth a kist of gold;

But if wet it be seen, Ere Holyrood e'en,

Bad harvest is foretold

'Seasons of mist and mellow fruitfulness' – who could put it better than Keats? Look out for Swallows lining up on telegraph wires preparing for their long journey south and the hedgerows turning white with Old Man's Beard, a type of wild clematis. The vernal equinox falls on 21 September, the point at which night and day are of equal length.

Michaelmas Day, also known as Goose Day, is on 29 September and is when Goose Fairs were held around the country. Holyrood Day, 14 September, also falls this month and commemorates the finding of the cross on which Christ was supposed to have suffered by Helena, mother of Emperor Constantine, in AD335.

Dry weather has always been important for bringing the harvest in – any dampness and the corn would all go mouldy. It is perhaps less important now that commercial grain driers are available, but a wet September can still be disastrous for farmers.

September

Spawning trout

Brown Trout (*Salmo trutta*) belong to the Salmonidae family, which includes salmon, charr and grayling. All these fish possess an adipose fin between the tail and the dorsal fin but it is not known what this is for.

Brown Trout remain in fresh water all their life but strangely some decide to go to sea and then become Sea Trout. Spawning takes place in the autumn or late autumn in northern latitudes. The trout find gravel beds with a good flow of water and the female or hen fish makes a trench in the gravel known as a 'redd' with her tail. She is joined by the male and as she lays her eggs he covers them with milt. Once fertilised the eggs absorb water and sink into the trench and the hen fish covers them with gravel. Not all eggs get covered and some will float off downstream to be eaten by other fish.

Trout feed on a wide variety of insects and also worms, small crustaceans and even grasshoppers. One of their favourite foods for the short time it appears is the mayfly.

Blackbird and Rowan

Male **Blackbirds** (*Turdus merula*), not unsurprisingly, have black plumage but the female is brown. A bright orange beak and eye ring make this an easy bird to recognise and its tuneful song is frequently heard in gardens.

Blackbirds feed on the ground, extracting worms from the soil and finding insects and berries. They are territorial birds, establishing their territories early in the year. Their nests are made of grass and twigs stuck together with mud, often untidy, hidden in hedges or bushes. Between three and five greenish-blue eggs are laid and incubated by the hen birds, although both parents will feed the young when they hatch.

The **Rowan** tree (*Sorbus aucuparia*), also called Mountain Ash, can grow at heights of up to 950 m, which is higher than any other native broadleaved tree – hence its name. The flowers appear in May to June and by September the berries are bright orange and much enjoyed by birds.

Rowan has all sorts of mythology and folklore attached to it: in Norse mythology it is the tree from which the first woman was made; in the UK it protects against witchcraft, indeed in Ireland and Scotland farmers would nail a branch to their cattle shed to protect their animals. The wood is strong and used for walking sticks (should you own one of these you will never get lost), tool handles and traditionally it is rowan wood that is used for making spinning wheels. Rowan berries can be made into jelly of a beautiful orange colour that is excellent with game.

September

Pink flowers

Watermint
(Menthe aquatic)

Knapweed
(Centaura nemaralis)

Peppermint
(Menthe piperita)

Common Mallow
(Malua sylvestris)

Cushion Calamint
(Clinopodium vulgare)

Hedgerow plants

Supposedly if you count the number of species in a hedge over a 10 m stretch and multiply by 100 you'll find out the age of the hedge – this is open to speculation, but it is true that some hedges are extremely old. One of the staple plants that makes for a stock-proof hedge is **Hawthorn** (*Crataegus monogyna*). Another is **Alder Buckthorn** (*Frangula alnus*), which has small bunches of white flowers in the spring that turn into blackberries in September. The leaves are the larval food of the Brimstone butterfly.

Another plant found in the hedgerow is **Spindle** (*Euonymus europaeus*). The tiny greenish-yellow flowers are hardly noticeable but this bush comes into its own when the poisonous fruit ripen into bright pink capsules with startlingly orange seeds. The wood is strong and smooth and was traditionally used to make knitting needles and spindles for spinning. On the continent it is used to fashion pipe-stems and it also makes excellent charcoal used for drawing.

Apart from giving character to the landscape and shelter for farm animals, hedges are an important source of food and refuge for a wide range of wild animals and birds.

September

How to make plaster of Paris animal tracks

First, of course, you will need to find a well-defined animal track. A good place to look is mud on the shore of a stream or pond, or any bare area in winter. It's possible to get prints from tracks in sand or even snow, but mud is the place to start.

YOU WILL NEED:

Packet of plaster of Paris

Mixing bowl

Measuring cup

Spoon

Strip of cardboard or bendy plastic about 20 cm × 40 cm, depending on the size of the track

Paper clips

Bottle of water

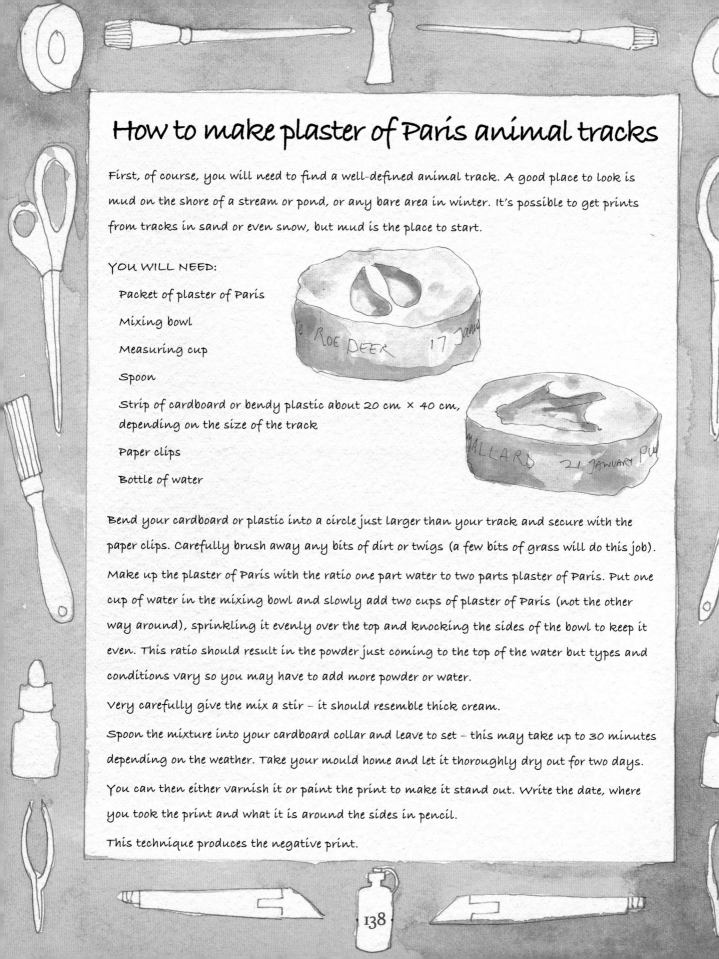

Bend your cardboard or plastic into a circle just larger than your track and secure with the paper clips. Carefully brush away any bits of dirt or twigs (a few bits of grass will do this job).

Make up the plaster of Paris with the ratio one part water to two parts plaster of Paris. Put one cup of water in the mixing bowl and slowly add two cups of plaster of Paris (not the other way around), sprinkling it evenly over the top and knocking the sides of the bowl to keep it even. This ratio should result in the powder just coming to the top of the water but types and conditions vary so you may have to add more powder or water.

Very carefully give the mix a stir – it should resemble thick cream.

Spoon the mixture into your cardboard collar and leave to set – this may take up to 30 minutes depending on the weather. Take your mould home and let it thoroughly dry out for two days.

You can then either varnish it or paint the print to make it stand out. Write the date, where you took the print and what it is around the sides in pencil.

This technique produces the negative print.

Common animal tracks

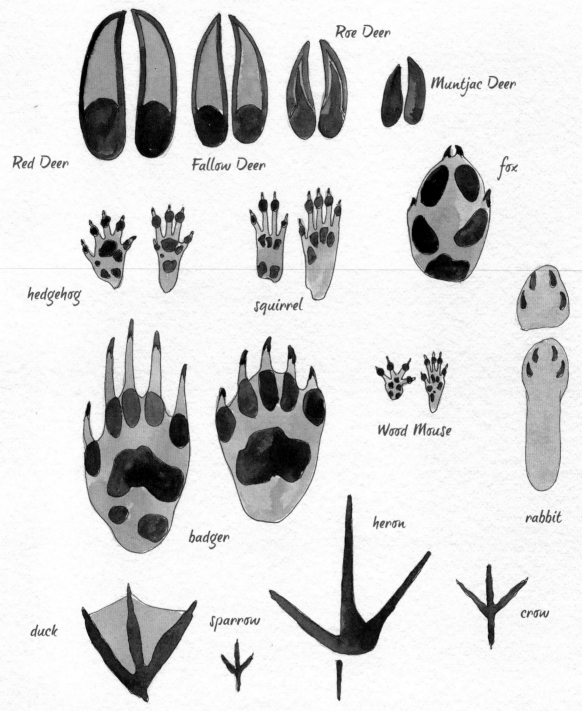

Roe Deer

Muntjac Deer

Red Deer

Fallow Deer

fox

hedgehog

squirrel

Wood Mouse

rabbit

badger

heron

crow

duck

sparrow

These paintings, of some of the animal tracks you might come across commonly on a walk, indicate (in the darker areas) the various pressure points each animal makes as it passes.

September

Barn Owl and Tawny Owl

Barn Owl

Barn Owls (*Tyto alba*) are nocturnal or crepuscular birds with a swooping graceful flight on silent wings. They hunt from the air, spotting small rodents on the ground in the dark. Generally they swallow their prey whole but, being unable to digest bones and hair, regurgitate a pellet. If you find a pile of these thumb-sized oblong balls you can see exactly what the owl has been eating.

On average a Barn Owl needs to catch about four small mammals every night – more during the breeding season when they're feeding their young. It might seem that owls are therefore controlling the numbers of voles and mice but in fact it is quite the opposite and the availability of small mammals dictates how many owls can live in a certain area.

Barn Owls like to nest, not unsurprisingly, in barns – before there were any they would have chosen crevices in cliffs and tree hollows. They don't build nests but find a level spot on which to lay their eggs. The eggs are laid two days apart, with the female starting to incubate immediately so that the eggs hatch two days apart as well. This is unfortunate for the youngest and therefore weakest owlet, but a clever ploy as it means that in lean hunting times the older owlets survive by eating their youngest sibling.

Tawny Owl

Tawny Owls (*Strix aluco*) are the owls that call the familiar 'too-wit too-woo', but this is in fact more correctly the female calling 'ke-wick' and the male answering 'hoo-hoo-hooo'. They have many other calls, including a screech, and are sometimes known as Screech Owls. Like the Barn Owl they feed on small mammals, start to incubate their eggs as they are laid, but prefer to nest in holes in trees.

Yellow flowers

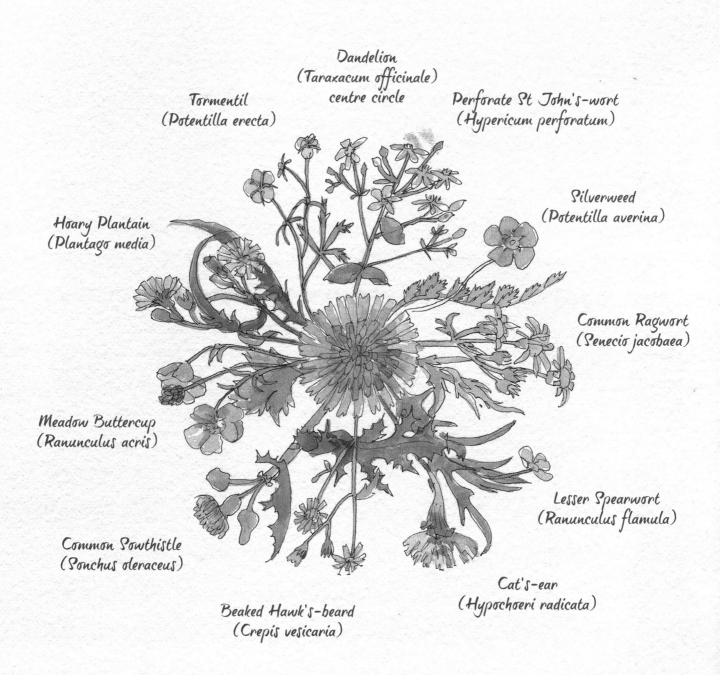

Dandelion
(Taraxacum officinale)
centre circle

Tormentil
(Potentilla erecta)

Perforate St John's-wort
(Hypericum perforatum)

Silverweed
(Potentilla averina)

Hoary Plantain
(Plantago media)

Common Ragwort
(Senecio jacobaea)

Meadow Buttercup
(Ranunculus acris)

Lesser Spearwort
(Ranunculus flamula)

Common Sowthistle
(Sonchus oleraceus)

Cat's-ear
(Hypochoeri radicata)

Beaked Hawk's-beard
(Crepis vesicaria)

Picked up on September walks

Pigeon's tail feather

Acorns

Beech mast

Pigeon's egg

Banded Snails
(Cepaea hortensis)

Garden Snail
(Helix aspersa)

Fruit of the Wild Arum

Great Spotted
Woodpecker feather

Fruit of the Wild Arum (*Arum maculatum*), also known as Cuckoo Pint or Lords and Ladies.
By September the leaves have died away, leaving the female flowers which have turned into
berries, green at first but then bright red. These berries are extremely poisonous.

September

Who ate the hazel nut?

You can learn a lot about which animals are around by having a closer look on the ground. Check under a hazel tree – you'll find a mass of old and broken nut shells, but who broke them open? In most cases if the nuts have been opened and jagged bits of shell remain the perpetrator is a squirrel, but you may also find nuts with neat round holes in them and these are made by mice. Look carefully and you can work out which type of mouse – the dormouse leaves the tidiest and roundest of holes and by looking at the teeth marks you'll be able to tell if it was the former, a Bank Vole or Wood Mouse.

Grey Squirrel
(Sciurus carolinensis)

Nut has been opened, with jagged bits of shell scattered around it.

Hazel Dormouse
(Muscardinus avellanarius)

Inner surface of hole smooth
and very round with tooth
marks on outside.

Bank Vole
(Myodes glareolus)

Tooth marks on inside of hole
and none on the outside.

Wood Mouse
(Apodemus sylvaticus)

Tooth marks on inside
and outside.

September

Is it a Buzzard, Red Kite, Kestrel or Sparrowhawk?

Buzzard

The **Buzzard** (*Buteo buteo*) is the most common bird of prey found all over the UK and Europe. Although not as large as a Golden Eagle, this is a big bird of prey, often seen sitting on telegraph poles or convenient branches from which to hunt. The plumage is variable in colour. Usually nesting in trees, the female lays between two and four eggs and incubation takes around 34 days. Buzzards feed on small mammals and birds as well as carrion. Look for splayed wing tips (fingers) when soaring, wedge-shaped tail and mournful mewing 'peeioo'.

Red Kite

The **Red Kite** (*Milvus milvus*) was almost completely exterminated in the UK by the late eighteenth century, although it remained plentiful on the Continent. However a reintroduction programme has been very successful and Red Kite numbers are gradually increasing.

The deeply forked tail is what gives the Red Kite away and distinguishes it from all other large raptors. The voice and soaring habit are similar to Buzzards and with a wingspan of nearly 2 meters and relatively small body these birds are capable of staying in the air for several hours with hardly a wing beat. They mate for life, with the female laying and incubating two to four eggs. While she is sitting on the eggs the female will be fed by the male – he will take his turn incubating for very short periods. The eggs are laid at three-day intervals and so also hatch at three-day intervals, meaning that the last to hatch is the smallest and is vulnerable if food is short – it may well be killed by its siblings.

Kestrel

Sparrowhawk

The **Kestrel** (*Falco tinnunculus*) is a small falcon with chestnut plumage, the male having a grey head and tail. The easiest way to distinguish them from a Sparrowhawk is to see them hovering and note the more pointed shape of the wings from the Sparrowhawk's rounded ones. Their call is a shrill 'kee-kee-kee', not unlike a Nuthatch. Kestrels nest in holes in trees or on ledges of cliffs or buildings. They feed on small mammals and have exceptionally good eyesight. They can also see ultraviolet light, which is useful for spotting voles that leave a trail of urine which glows in ultraviolet light.

The **Sparrowhawk** (*Accipiter nisus*) male is slate grey and the larger female a slightly browner grey. Their characteristic flight is a dash between trees or over a hedge to grab their prey, frequently birds that they then pluck alive, standing with both feet on their victim and wings held forwards as if hiding it.

September

RECIPE

Wild plum and damson chutney

The joy of chutney is that anything can go in and it doesn't have to set so measurements are less important than with jelly. Most wild fruit is sour so this chutney does have a lot of sugar in it, but that can also be altered to taste.

Damsons and wild plums have stones that need to be removed – the easiest way to do this is to pre-cook the fruit in the vinegar. The fruit will pop open and the stones will float to the top to be removed with a slotted spoon. Count the fruit as it goes in and then count the stones as they come out to make sure you've got them all!

YOU WILL NEED:

1 kg plums or damsons (you can add rowan berries, blackberries, elderberries, whatever you can find at the time), stoned

250 g onions, chopped

250 g sultanas

1 inch (2.5 cm) piece of ginger, chopped finely

3 cloves garlic, chopped

500 g brown sugar (demerara, soft brown, or a mixture)

500 ml vinegar (white wine or malt)

any other spices you fancy – cinnamon, allspice, star anise

jars and lids or jam pot covers

Place all the ingredients in a heavy-based pan and simmer slowly, stirring occasionally, until the vinegar has reduced by approximately a third and the mixture appears syrupy – this should take about 40 minutes.

While the chutney is simmering put your jars into a moderate oven and when the chutney is ready pour it into the hot jars. Cover with waxed sealing discs and seal with a cellophane disc or a jar lid.

Makes about six to eight 1 lb jars. Chutney improves with age so store for 3 months in a dark cupboard before using.

Lombardy Poplar

TYPE *Populous nigra* is a tall, deciduous, fast-growing tree with upwardly pointing branches giving it a columnar shape. Very tolerant to cold and dry climates. Introduced from Italy.

SIZE 20–35 m.

BARK Pale bark with deep fissures and sometimes burrs from which twigs sprout.

FOLIAGE Shiny triangular turning to bright yellow in autumn.

FRUIT AND FLOWERS The Lombardy Poplar is male only but produces red catkins.

USES Typically planted along European roads to create shade. Poplar wood is soft and light but does not swell or shrink and is used to make such things as butcher's trays, animal troughs and other things where cost and lightness are more important than durability. In Holland poplar is made into clogs.

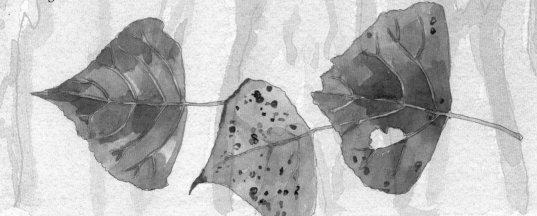

October

Fine weather when the geese fly high,

When flying low a storm is nigh

Squirrels and Jays will be very busy this month, hiding acorns and other nuts to recover later in the winter when food is short. Animals that hibernate will be searching out safe havens. Look out for the ubiquitous Fly Agaric with its startling red and white spotted cap.

Geese and other water birds will be returning from their summer breeding grounds in the Arctic – Barnacle Geese in particular to the Solway Firth but also to the islands of Scotland and Ireland, Islay being particularly popular. Brent Geese, Pink-footed Geese and Greylag Geese all come further south to estuaries, feeding on crops in adjoining fields.

Look out for the earth star fungus (*Geastrum triplex*), which starts life as a rather indistinct round ball and then puffs into a delightful star shape – there are many types of earth star, all rather rare, but this is the most common and can be found in leaf litter in deciduous woods.

October

Fungi

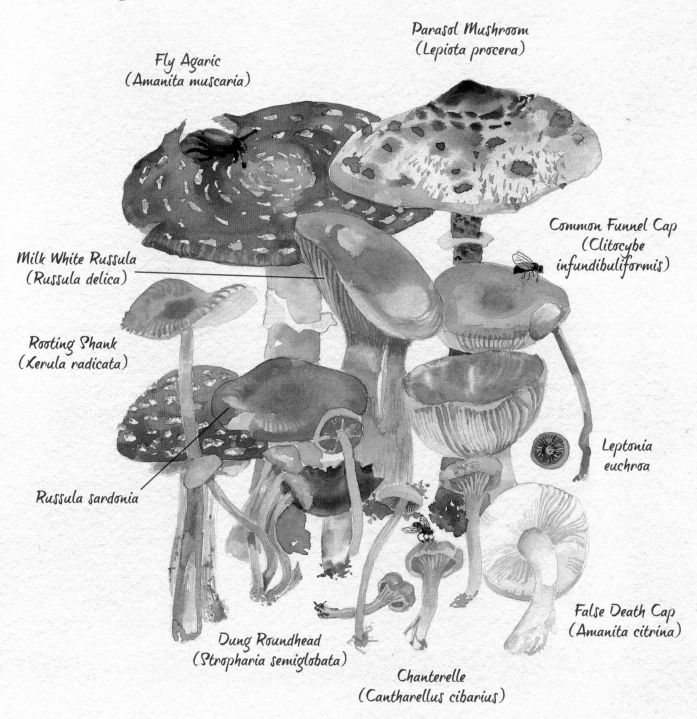

Fly Agaric
(Amanita muscaria)

Parasol Mushroom
(Lepiota procera)

Common Funnel Cap
(Clitocybe infundibuliformis)

Milk White Russula
(Russula delica)

Rooting Shank
(Xerula radicata)

Leptonia euchroa

Russula sardonia

False Death Cap
(Amanita citrina)

Dung Roundhead
(Stropharia semiglobata)

Chanterelle
(Cantharellus cibarius)

Horse Chestnut

The Horse Chestnut (*Aesculus hippocastanum*) is a large ornamental, deciduous tree more commonly best known as a 'conker tree' after its fruit. It is known for the game of 'conkers', which was invented in the late eighteenth century. Conkers have regional names such as 'obblyonkers', 'cheggies' and 'cheesers'.

- The Horse Chestnut was introduced to Britain from the Balkans in the late sixteenth century.
- The Horse Chestnut flowers in April/May and produces fruit called conkers in September/October.
- Unsurprisingly, given the tree's name, conkers were once fed to horses to make their coats shine.
- However conkers contain aesculin, a toxin poisonous to humans and some animals.
- The leaves have five to seven leaflets and the large upright flowers are known as 'candles'.
- When the leaf falls off it leaves behind a horseshoe-shaped scar with seven nail holes on the twigs.
- In the house conkers are used to discourage moths and spiders.
- Kept in a pocket a conker is said to prevent piles and rheumatism.
- Used in Europe to whiten hemp, flax, silk and wool, because when it is crushed in water it emits a soapy juice.
- The flower is the symbol of the city of Kiev.
- A close relative (*Aesculus glabra*) is known as buckeye in the USA.
- Native Americans were able to roast buckeyes and leach out the toxin to render the conkers edible.
- They also used the ground fruit as a powder on shallow water to stun and catch fish.

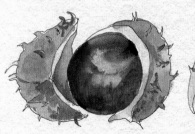

Which swan is it?

Whooper Swan

Bewick's Swan

Mute Swan

Arguably the most elegant and beautiful of waterfowl, swans dip their long necks into water to feed on the weed at the bottom and also graze on shore grasses. In large groups they fly in a V-formation but where there are few they can be seen in lines.

Mute Swan

The **Mute Swan** (*Cygnus olor*) is the most numerous of the swans and also semi-domesticated. They breed and overwinter in the UK. When swimming the neck is held in a graceful curve with the orange bill with black knob pointing down.

The **Bewick's Swan** (*Cygnus bewickii*) is a winter visitor to its UK wetland habitat from Siberia and the smallest of the swans. Rather similar to the Whooper Swan but smaller with a shorter neck and more rounded head.

The pattern on the bill varies from bird to bird but always has more black than yellow.

The **Whooper Swan** (*Cygnus cygnus*) is more common than the Bewick's and is also a winter visitor to the UK. It has a characteristic straight neck carriage and differs from the Bewick in that it is larger and has more yellow than black on its bill. The Whooper Swan is also noisier, with a whooping call that carries over long distances.

Whooper Swan

Ivy

Ivy provides the last of the nectar and pollen of the year for bees and will also attract butterflies. One that particularly seems to enjoy it is the Red Admiral (*Vanessa atalanta*), a migratory species found all over Europe. Not many survive the winter but the species is replenished in the spring with visitors from North Africa, which will produce a second generation in the UK and Europe.

Who ate the fir cone?

Mature fir cone – wet

Cone eaten by squirrel
(resembles apple core)

Mature fir cone – dry

Young cone

Cone eaten by woodpecker
(mangled)

Red Fox

Found over the entire northern hemisphere, the Red Fox (*Vulpes vulpes*) is the most widely distributed of all wild carnivores and the only large carnivore that has successfully colonised urban and suburban areas.

Foxes live on rodents, rabbits, birds, birds' eggs and even frogs and worms. In urban areas they raid dustbins and spread disease; on the continent they also carry rabies. They are skilful and destructive killers and a great nuisance to anyone who wishes to keep poultry.

Mating takes place in the winter, when barking and unearthly screams can be heard, and the vixen gives birth in an earth to litters numbering up to ten but more usually four or five. Both parents look after the cubs, the vixen remaining with them for the first two weeks and relying on the dog fox to feed her. In the autumn the well-grown cubs leave their home to find territories of their own.

What type of thrush is it?

The thrush family belong to the genus *Turdus* which, as well as Mistle and Song Thrushes, includes the Redwing and Fieldfare as well as the Blackbird, with its distinctive glossy black plumage and bright orange eyes.

Redwing

The **Redwing** (*Turdus iliacus*) (21 cm) is the smallest thrush and is easy to spot by its chestnut red underwing, which is most obvious in flight. Like the Fieldfare, Redwings feed on invertebrates, berries and fruit, and can be seen in large numbers in autumn as they migrate south, sometimes stripping holly trees of every berry. Their voice is a quiet high-pitched 'seep'. They are a winter visitor to the UK from their summer breeding grounds in Iceland, Scandinavia and Russia.

The **Mistle Thrush** (*Turdus viscivorus*) (27 cm) is larger than the Song Thrush with more obvious spots. The sexes are alike. Its voice is a harsh churring chatter. Like the Song Thrush it hammers snails on an anvil but also eats berries and fruit.

Mistle Thrush

The **Fieldfare** (*Turdus pilaris*) (25 cm) has a slate grey head, nape and rump. The female is similar but duller in colour. Fieldfares have a harsh chattering call and feed on invertebrates, berries and fruit. They are a winter visitor to UK and can be seen in large flocks, sometimes teaming up with Redwings as they migrate south.

Fieldfare

October

How to print cards with natural objects

You can print using all sorts of things – flowers, feathers, leaves, lichen – in fact the sky's the limit. Skeleton leaves have a beauty all their own and make beautiful greeting cards. First find your leaves. At this time of year all the leaves will be on the ground, simply look around and find some that have rotted over the previous winter leaving just the veins – holly leaves work particularly well.

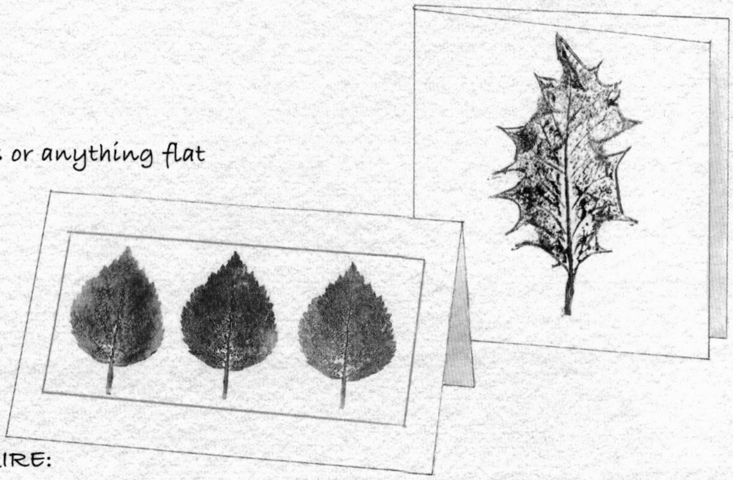

YOU WILL NEED:

Leaves, feathers, flowers, ferns or anything flat

Printing ink

Paintbrush

Newspaper

Rolling pin, bottle or spoon

METHOD 2 WILL ALSO REQUIRE:

Two sheets of plastic, glass or acrylic

Roller (brayer)

Card

The best results will be achieved by using etching or lino printing ink but poster paint will also work. Here are two ways of taking prints:

METHOD 1: simply paint the leaf with your chosen ink, lay it very carefully on your card, cover with a piece of newspaper and roll with a rolling pin or bottle or just burnish with a wooden spoon. This method takes a bit of practice in order not to cause the leaf to shift and smudge.

METHOD 2: this sounds more complicated but will achieve better results. You will need a sheet of plastic, small piece of glass or piece of acrylic. Either paint or use a roller to apply the ink to your surface, place the leaf or as many leaves as you can fit on at once, cover with newspaper and roll as above. Now carefully lift the leaf (tweezers might help), and place it ink side down on your card, cover with newspaper and roll again.

October

Crab apple jelly

Crab apples make the most delicious jelly, mainly thanks to the fact that they are so sour, although all jellies require a great deal of sugar. This crab apple jelly will be a delightful pink colour and can be varied in several different ways, as explained below.

Wash 2 kg crab apples and chop them in half.

Place in a large jam pan or saucepan.

Cover with water and bring to the boil.

Boil until turned to a pulp – 20–30 minutes.

Strain through a jelly bag, leaving overnight and resisting the temptation to squeeze the bag as this will make your jelly cloudy.

Measure juice and for every 1 pt (500 ml) add 1 lb (450 g) sugar.

Return to the pan and boil until setting point is reached.*

Allow to cool for a few moments, then pour into sterilised hot jars and cover with jam pot covers.

VARIATIONS:

Add rowan berries or sloes to the apples to cook.

Put a sprig of rosemary in when bottling.

Add chopped mint when setting point is reached, leave to cool slightly and stir carefully before putting in jars.

Add chilli powder or chopped chillies as above.

*To test for setting point put a saucer in the fridge before you begin. At first your jelly will froth in the saucepan, but when it stops doing this tip a teaspoon-full onto the cold saucer and then push it with your finger – if the jelly wrinkles and stays where you've pushed, it rather than running back, it is ready.

Hornbeam

TYPE *Carpinus betulus* is a native deciduous broadleaf tree found throughout Europe and most common in southern Britain and not found above 600 m.

SIZE 10–25 m.

BARK Smooth grey with vertical stripes.

FOLIAGE Markedly serrated leaves with 10–14 pairs of veins on each leaf.

FLOWERS AND SEEDS Catkins that appear in May and June and develop into large winged keys.

USES Very hard wood, which explains its name ('horn' meaning 'hard'). It's also sometimes known as ironwood. Being hard it is difficult to work with but it is ideal for such things as ox yokes, pulleys, mallets, skittles and chopping blocks. It's also valued for fuel as it is slow burning and gives off a lot of heat. It's thought that the maze hedges at Hampton Court were originally hornbeam, before being replaced with yew.

October

November

If there's ice in November that will bear a duck,
There'll be nothing after but sludge and muck.

Along with the red berries of Holly and Hawthorn you may spot the bright scarlet berries of White Bryony (*Bryonia dioica*) twining its way along fences or in bushy shrubs. Strangely this is a member of the cucumber family, but these berries are not for eating. In the fourteenth century it was used as an antidote to leprosy – it is in fact a very strong laxative.

Most of the leaves will be on the ground by now but if you're lucky you may spot a Woodcock. Most of these attractive birds are resident in the UK but their numbers are swelled at this time of year by birds moving south from Finland and Russia to overwinter in our less harsh climate. Beautifully camouflaged, this is a hard bird to spot but if you disturb one it will leap into the air and zigzag away through the trees. In spring the males perform a special kind of flight known as 'roding', when they follow a particular route while uttering a strange croaking sound – this takes place just after sunset and directly before sunrise.

Woodpigeon

Should you come across a large pile of grey feathers on the ground, this is most likely to be where an unfortunate Woodpigeon (*Columba palumbus*) has been caught by a Sparrowhawk, which has immediately plucked the bird on the spot. Peregrine Falcons also favour pigeons as a meal.

Pigeons build a fairly careless nest of twigs but once the one or two eggs are laid, both parents take it in turn to incubate and so the eggs are never left exposed. The eggs hatch in around 18 days and a couple of days before hatching both parents start to produce milk – not really milk, of course, but a secretion specially designed to feed the young. The parent bird regurgitates the milk, which is made in the crop, and the chicks grow fast on this high protein food. Gradually the parents introduce seeds and greens and finally stop producing milk, by which time the squab, as young pigeons are known, feeds normally.

Pigeons are very good parents and look after their young for longer than most birds, which gives the juveniles a better chance of survival. They can have up to two or three broods a year.

The crop of a full-grown pigeon can contain a large amount of food – what is shown here is typical for a pigeon at this time of year.

Is it a Weasel or a Stoat?

Stoat

Everyone knows that a weasel is weasily distinguished and a stoat is stoatally different but in reality it is hard to tell. They have many features in common, both being carnivorous, feeding on bird's eggs, small mammals such as mice and voles as well as rabbits. They both live in dens, often moving into the home of their prey and using the prey's fur to line their nests.

But there are also ways to tell them apart. **Stoats** (*Mustela erminea*) are significantly larger (male 27–31 cm, female 24–29 cm) than **Weasels** (*Mustela nivalis*) (male 19–20 cm, female 17–18 cm). The Stoat has a black tip to its tail, while the Weasel has a short tail with no black tip. Weasels are gingery brown with a cream belly; stoats are reddish-brown to ginger with a white belly. In the north the Stoat may turn white in winter, when they are called ermine, retaining only its black tip to its tail.

Both are widespread, although Weasels are not found at high altitude.

Weasels give birth to two litters of four to six kits, while Stoats have one litter of six to twelve kits.

Weasel

November

Badger

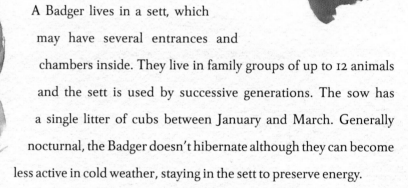

Although the Badger (*Meles meles*) looks like a bear, with its strong bear-like clawed paws, it does in fact belong to the weasel family. Commonly called 'brock', the Badger is an omnivore, feeding mainly on earthworms, small mammals, insects, bulbs, berries and even lizards. It lives for up to 14 years and weighs in at 8–12 kg, measuring 65–80 cm from tail to tip of snout.

A Badger lives in a sett, which may have several entrances and chambers inside. They live in family groups of up to 12 animals and the sett is used by successive generations. The sow has a single litter of cubs between January and March. Generally nocturnal, the Badger doesn't hibernate although they can become less active in cold weather, staying in the sett to preserve energy.

Signs of Badgers include piles of discarded bedding in autumn near the sett, latrines, scratched bark and paths leading away. Look for the telltale black-and-white hairs that may be stuck in the entrances. If you want to see Badgers emerge from their sett you will have to approach well before dusk and keep extremely still and quiet.

Badgers have no predators apart from humans, but are frequently killed on roads or culled as, sadly, they have the reputation of carrying bovine tuberculosis.

In countryside where Badgers and stone walls coincide, sensible farmers incorporate Badger gaps in their walls – this is because otherwise the badger would simply destroy any wall built over one of its routes.

Droppings and pellets

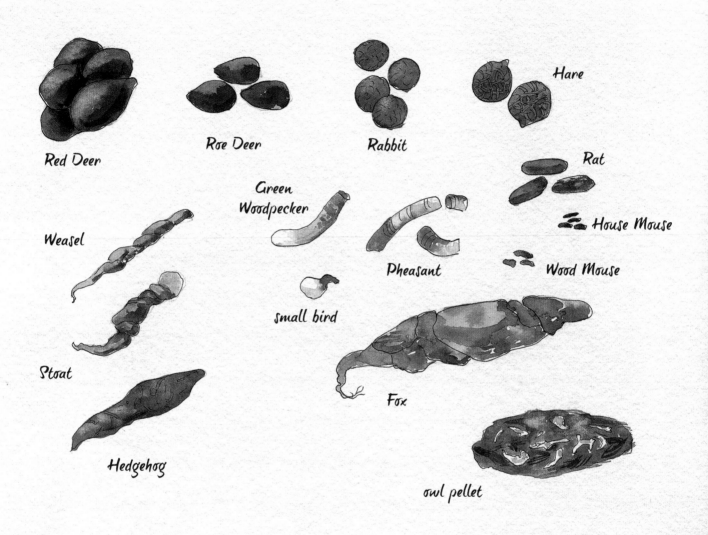

Red Deer

Roe Deer

Rabbit

Hare

Green Woodpecker

Weasel

Rat

House Mouse

Pheasant

Wood Mouse

Stoat

small bird

Fox

Hedgehog

owl pellet

Recognising droppings (although perhaps initially distasteful) is an excellent way of finding out what is about. You may not see a nocturnal hedgehog but if you can recognise its droppings you will know one is around and it might be worth a night-time prowl to see if you can find it.

Several birds cough up pellets that are the undigestible remains of their diet, such things as bones, hair or beetle shells, which form into a ball and are regurgitated. Looking into an owl's pellet is fascinating as you can see the tiny jawbones of mice and all sorts of other little bits and pieces and work out what the owl has been feeding on.

November

Polypores

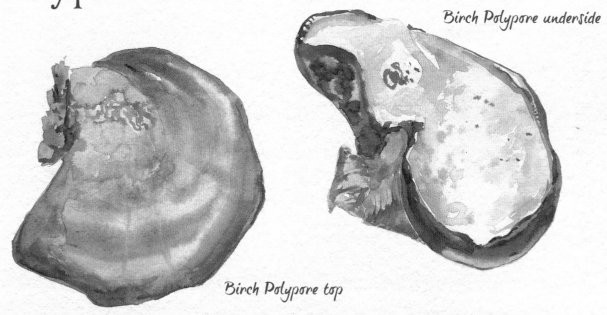

Birch Polypore underside

Birch Polypore top

Also known as razor strop or birch bracket, Birch Polypore (*Piptoporus betulinus*) occurs only on dead or dying birch trees. It is very common and can be seen growing out of the trunks as a hoof-like shelf. The brackets can measure up to 25 cm and although an annual they are so tough that some will be visible at any time of year.

Although not poisonous, this fungus is inedible. But it does have its uses. As its alternative name suggests, it was once used to strop razors and when dried can be used as a firelighter. In fact Otzi, the 5,000-year-old man found in a glacier in the Tyrol, was carrying some in a bag, presumably to use as tinder.

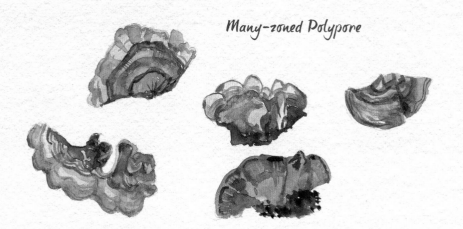

Many-zoned Polypore

Many-zoned Polypore (*Coriolus versicolor*) is found all over the world on dead and dying trees, particularly beech. Its shape and striped colouring giving it the nickname 'turkey tail'.

How to make a fungus fish

Many-zoned Polypore is a common fungus that grows on dead trees and is just the right size and shape to make fish scales. You can use them to make this fun fungus fish.

YOU WILL NEED:

20–25 pieces polypore fungus

Silver birch bark

A few twigs

An acorn cup

Insecticide aerosol
(moth or fly killer)

Plastic bag

Piece of MDF, plywood or cardboard
to make template

Strong glue

Varnish

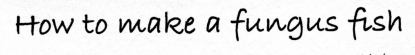

First find about 20–25 pieces of fungus and put them in a plastic bag. Spray the insecticide into the plastic bag and tie the top tightly – you don't want to bring any wood-boring bugs into your house – and leave overnight. Repeat this step the next day, just to be sure.

Place your polypores on a tray and leave them somewhere warm to thoroughly dry out – this may take up to a week.

Make a fish-shaped template and cut out your fish base – it could be MDF, plywood or even cardboard (if you use cardboard cut out two templates and glue them together for strength).

Cut your birch bark to fit the head, fins and tail (you can do this with scissors) and glue in place – leave to dry with a weight on top or use bulldog clips.

Using strong glue liberally, stick your dried polypore scales onto the fish shape, starting at the tail and overlapping as you go.

Stick the twigs on the tail and the acorn cup to form the eye.

Finish by giving the whole thing a couple of coats of varnish.

Chestnut and mushroom loaf

This really is a meal in itself, or you could serve it as a most unusual accompaniment to any meat dish.

If you're lucky enough to find some field mushrooms make absolutely sure that that is what they are – beautiful pink or dark brown gills, never white. If you're in any doubt it's safer to buy them!

Peeling chestnuts is a fiddly business – the easiest way is to make a cut in one side and then boil them for 10 to 15 minutes until cooked, peeling them before they cool.

YOU WILL NEED:

250 g peeled chestnuts

3 onions, finely chopped

2 cloves garlic, finely chopped

500 g mushrooms, chopped

125 g dried cranberries
(or use rowan berries if the birds
haven't eaten them all)

1 egg

a few sage leaves

2 tbsp Worcester sauce

salt and pepper

Preheat the oven to 200C.

In a heavy-based pan fry the onions in oil until almost cooked, add the garlic and mushrooms and continue to sauté for another 10 minutes or so until just cooked.

Put all the ingredients into a food processor and whizz until combined but not over smooth.

Tip into a 1 lb (450 g) non-stick loaf tin, cover with foil and bake in the oven for 25 minutes, removing the foil for the last 10 minutes.

The loaf will be firmer if allowed to cool, but serve hot or cold as desired. Serves 4–6.

Horse Chestnut

TYPE *Aesculus hippocastanum* is a broadleaf deciduous tree introduced to the UK from south-east Europe in the late sixteenth century.

SIZE 14–30 m.

BARK Smooth pinky-grey with horseshoe-shaped marks on the twigs left by leaves from the previous year.

FOLIAGE The leaf bud, known as a sticky bud, is reddish-brown and indeed sticky. The leaves have seven (but occasionally five or six) leaflets on one central stem.

FLOWERS AND SEEDS Large multiple flower spikes known as 'candles' up to 20 cm in height. Shiny chestnut-coloured conker inside a green spiky case.

USES The timber is of little value, being soft and pulpy, and this tree is generally grown for its beauty and shade.

November

December

If Christmas day be bright and clear

There'll be two winters in the year

This month brings the shortest day, after which the evenings will at last begin to draw out. One of our best-loved mammals, the Red Squirrel (*Sciurus vulgaris*), can be seen in its native pine woods as they do not hibernate. Unfortunately they have an increasingly uncertain future thanks to the introduction of the American Grey Squirrel.

Red Squirrels have bushy tails and tufted ears that are moulted once a year. Reds build large dreys to give birth in and provide shelter in cold weather. They are primarily seed eaters although also enjoy fungi, berries and bark. They store surplus food in gaps in tree bark or underground for use during the winter.

Mistletoe (*Viscum album*) is a parasitic plant that grows on deciduous trees, particularly favouring apple. It was an ancient fertility symbol, hence the tradition of kissing under it at Christmas, and was a sign of good luck to the druids. Although poisonous the sticky white berries are thought to have anti-cancer properties and mistletoe tea, made from the dried leaves, is thought to lower high blood pressure.

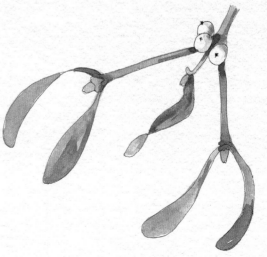

December

Robin and Holly

Easily recognised by their spiny glossy leaves, **Holly** trees (*Ilex aquifolium*) are either male or female. The small, insignificant white flowers turn first into green berries, becoming bright red as winter progresses, and although slightly poisonous to humans provide a valuable food source for birds, including Robins.

Male and female **Robins** (*Erithacus rubecula*) are difficult to distinguish from each other although the juvenile starts life speckled. Robins nest near to the ground in whatever they come across, which may be such extraordinary things as abandoned teapots or letter boxes. They are pugnacious little birds that bravely guard their territories. In winter the hen develops a separate area or 'estate' of her own. Unlike most birds, Robins sing in winter, but it is probably their red breasts – similar to that of Father Christmas – that make them synonymous with this time of year.

Picked up on a winter walk

Yellow brain fungus
(Tremella mesenterica)

A jelly-like mass that appears on dead deciduous branches sometimes still attached to the tree. The fungus is golden-yellow at first, becoming more orange with age and drying to a dark orange horny lump.

Roe Deer antler

Piece of wood

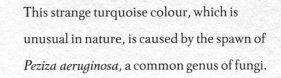

This strange turquoise colour, which is unusual in nature, is caused by the spawn of *Peziza aeruginosa*, a common genus of fungi.

This is the time of year Roe Deer shed their antlers and so is the most likely time to come across one.

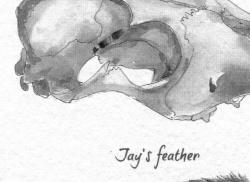

Fox skull

Jay's feather

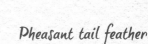

Three cones: Scots Pine, larch and alder

Pheasant tail feather

December

Wren and Ivy

Ivy (*Hedera helix*) is a climbing plant that can reach heights of 30 m. It has two leaf types – palmate-lobed young leaves on the climbing stems and unlobed cordate adult leaves on the flowering stems. The flowers bloom in autumn to early winter, producing copious amounts of nectar which attracts bees and butterflies as most other flowers are long gone by this time of year. The fruit is green, gradually turning to purple-black, and is a valuable food source for birds, like Wrens, who also nest and roost in the safety of the leaves.

Wrens (*Troglodytes troglodytes*) are busy little birds found all over the UK and Europe. Probably the first sign that a Wren is nearby will be the sharp alarm call, which is remarkably loud for such a small bird, followed by a brown flash as it darts about low to the ground. When perched look out for their distinctive cocked tail which they flick repeatedly. Wrens feed on insects and spiders and the population can be devastated by a severe winter as they must eat constantly to maintain their tiny frames.

What type of tit is it?

Blue Tit

Great Tit

Marsh Tit

Coal Tit

Long-tailed Tit

The **Blue Tit** (*Parus caeruleus*) is the most common of the tits and easy to recognise by its blue cap and yellow breast. This is a sociable bird that gangs up with other types of tit as well as Goldcrests and warblers in winter. It is the most likely occupant of your nest box.

The **Great Tit** (*Parus major*) is the largest of the tits, with a black head, white cheeks and yellow body with a smart black bib.

The **Long-tailed Tit** (*Aegithalos caudatus*) is unmistakable with its black and pink body, white crown and exaggeratedly long tail. You're most likely to encounter it in woodland, sometimes in large numbers and with other breeds of tit.

The **Coal Tit** (*Parus ater*) is black and grey with white cheeks, and has a white stripe on the back of its black head which distinguishes it from the Marsh Tit.

The **Marsh Tit** (*Parus palustris*) is similar in appearance to the Coal Tit but sleeker, with a glossy crown and it lacks the white stripe on the nape.

December

How to make feather (and other) earrings

Keep your eyes peeled while out for a walk for suitable objects – once you start looking it's amazing how many feathers are dropped by birds. You might find beautiful blue ones from a Jay's wing or grey ones from a pigeon. Look by a pond where ducks have been preening – another good source is the high tide line on a beach.

YOU WILL NEED:

A pair of ear hooks and pinch catches (these look like little clams) (both available at craft shops known as 'findings')

Matching feathers

Drop of glue

First find your matching feathers – you could use one, two or a whole bunch. Almost any feather is suitable – pheasants have absolutely gorgeous ones and if you can find a couple of the jewel-like blue wing feathers from a Jay you can't go wrong.

Clean off a bit of the fluff from the bottom of the feathers, put a drip of glue into the pinch catch, squeeze it shut on the feather, attach the ear hook – that's it done!

Acorns make delightful earrings or pendants but they do tend to wrinkle when totally dry, but for short-term wear all you need is a pair of ear hooks and a couple of findings called 'filigree caps' that you squeeze onto the top of the acorn – a drop of glue would keep them secure.

You can even make earrings out of fungus. Cure the fungus in the same way as for the fungus fish on page 171 and pinch on a finding known as a 'prong bail' using pliers. Give the fungus several coats of varnish – beautiful.

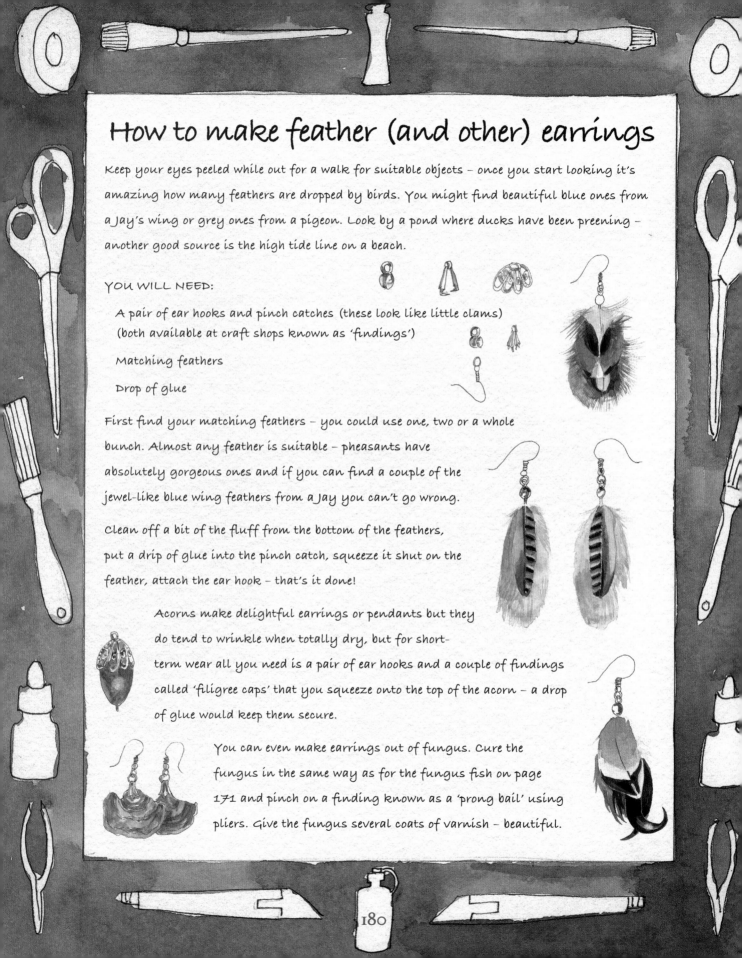

Canada Goose

The handsome Canada Goose (*Branta canadensis*) was introduced from North America and has adapted very successfully to Europe, in fact in some places it is now so numerous that it is considered a nuisance. The first birds were imported in 1665 as exotic additions to the wildfowl collection of King Charles II in St James Park, but it wasn't until the last century that they really began to breed in the wild.

Adult birds mate for life and typically raise five goslings. The goose incubates the eggs with the gander standing guard and both birds raise the young. This is a large goose with a wingspan of 180 cm that can live for up to 30 years, although the average is lifespan is 15–20 years.

Mandarin Duck

The beautiful Mandarin Duck (*Aix galericulata*) is not native to the UK but has successfully established itself all over the country from escapees of waterfowl collections. It lives close to streams and ponds with wooded edges and unusually nests in tree holes. When the ducklings hatch the duck flies down to the ground and calls to her progeny until they leap from their nest, bouncing as they land undamaged. She leads them to water where her mate will be waiting to help raise the young.

December

Feathers found on the ground

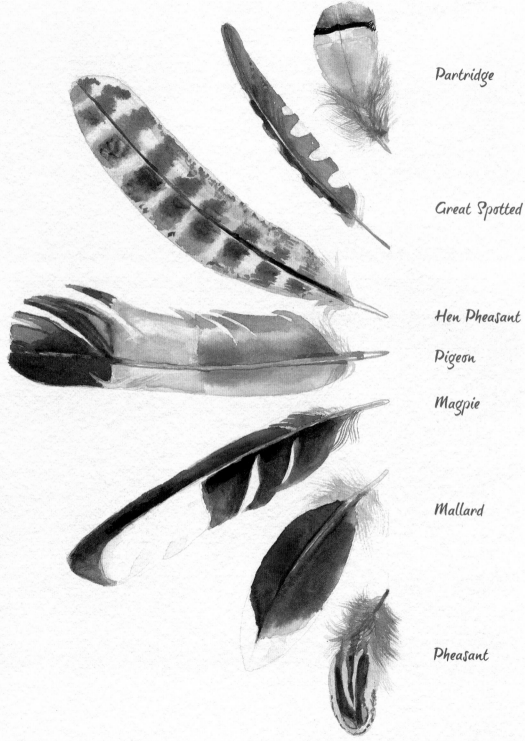

Partridge

Great Spotted Woodpecker

Hen Pheasant

Pigeon

Magpie

Mallard

Pheasant

Treecreeper and Nuthatch

The **Treecreeper** (*Certhia familiaris*) is a charming little bird that lives amongst trees, working its way up the trunk and along branches in rather mouse-like hops and runs, then dropping down to the foot of the next tree. The curved beak and creeping movement are the things to look out for. At only about 12 cm in length this is a bird that suffers in hard winters because it lives exclusively on small bark insects. Both sexes build the nest, either in a tree crevice or sometimes in ivy, and both incubate and feed the young.

Nuthatches (*Sitta europaea*) are slightly larger and stouter than Treecreepers. They are the only bird that habitually goes down trees headfirst (at one time it was even thought to sleep head down – but this may be an old wive's tale) and can be seen going up and down the trunk with jerky dashes. The nest is made in a tree hole, with the entrance reduced to the correct size with beakfuls of mud.

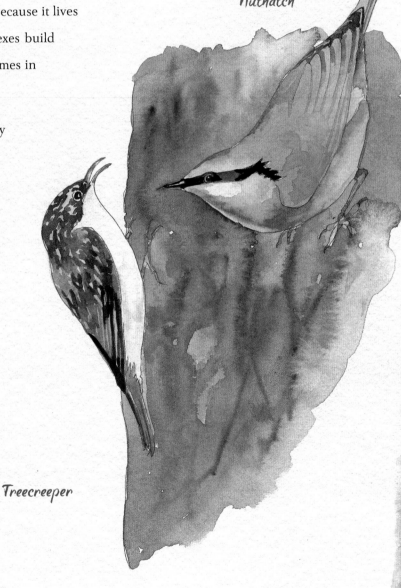

Nuthatch

Treecreeper

Moles

Moles produce the molehills much bemoaned by gardeners. Although moles live underground they do come up to the surface occasionally, particularly the young, in order to search for new territory.

- Moles have tiny or invisible eyes and ears but a powerful sense of smell.

- They have short, powerful front legs with large paws for digging.

- The mole finds its way about its tunnels by signals produced by 'vibrissae', the sensitive hairs on its face, feet and tail, and 'Elmer's organs', which are tiny papillae on the end of the mole's nose.

- The mole's fur can lie at any angle, allowing it to go backwards as well as forwards through its tunnels.

- Moles build a single chamber with interconnecting tunnels and can dig 30 m of new tunnel in 24 hours.

- Moles are found from sea level to high altitude in all kinds of soil but it is rare to see one above ground.

- Moles are mainly solitary, apart from when mating and rearing young.

- They are carnivorous – a mole eats its own body weight per day.

- Their favourite food is earthworms, but they will also eat insect larvae and other invertebrates. When food is plentiful the mole will bite and paralyse its prey, storing it in its chamber until needed.

- If moles feed entirely on worms they do not need to drink as worms are 85% water.

- Moles make various noises, including squeaks and purrs.

- The normal litter size is three, they only have one litter per year and weaning takes place at 31 days.

- The mole's gestation period is 28 days.

- Moles live for between 3 and 5 years.

- The mole is also called the moldwarp.

Lapwing

Also known as the Green Plover, or Peewit, the name Lapwing derives from their springtime aerial displays, when their wings make a loud lapping noise. Their call of 'pee-wit, pee-wit' explains another of their common names.

Lapwings (*Vanellus vanellus*) are gregarious and generally live in large flocks outside the breeding season, sometimes joining up with other waders or starlings. They frequent farmland and breed in damp rushy fields and coastal marshes, building a shallow nest on the ground. The chicks are precocial and able to feed themselves immediately on worms and insects, with both parents caring for them.

Some Lapwings are resident and some migrate west or south, but many more arrive on the east coast in autumn from the continent.

December

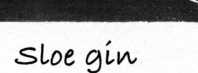

Sloe gin

Sloes are the fruit of the blackthorn – a common hedgerow plant. Although too sour to eat they add a delightful fruity flavour to gin. Traditionally they should not be harvested until after the first frost of the winter. The almonds are optional but add depth to the finished liqueur.

YOU WILL NEED:

For a 1 litre bottle of gin add:

  500 g sloes, pricked all over

  300 g granulated sugar

  Eight almonds (or three drops almond essence)

In a 2 litre preserving jar (you can just use bottles but that makes retrieving the sloes at a later date very difficult) add a layer of pricked sloes, then sugar and an almond, and continue in layers until all the fruit and sugar is used up. Pour over the gin and cover the jar securely. Put in a cool dark place.

Shake the jar whenever you are passing (or at least two or three times a week) for 3 months and then leave for a further 6 months. Strain the liquid and pour into bottles through a funnel. Don't forget to add a label with the vintage date!

No need to waste the gin-soaked fruit – squeeze the stones out, melt some dark chocolate, add the fruit – you've made an unusual liqueur chocolate.

Yew

TYPE *Taxus baccata* is a native evergreen conifer, the leaves and berries of which are extremely poisonous, although the leaves are now used to produce a drug that inhibits cancer cell growth.

SIZE 4–20 m

BARK Scaly and colourful, ranging from purple through red to grey.

FOLIAGE Dark green flat needles arranged either side of the twig.

FLOWERS AND SEEDS Small flowers in early spring that develop into red berries.

USES Traditionally used for longbows and spears as although heavy it is very elastic. The timber is so hard it's said a fence post made of yew will outlast one made of iron.

No one knows why yews were planted in churchyards but there are over 500 churchyards in the UK which contain yews older than the church itself. The beautiful chestnut-brown colour and groups of pin knots and fine texture of the timber also make it sought after for furniture construction.

December

Useful websites

www.britishbirdphotographs.com

Wonderful selection of bird photographs by Barry Boswell.

www.nhm.ac.uk

The comprehensive site of the Natural History Museum covering millennia of information.

www.uklichens.co.uk

Everything you ever wanted to know about lichens found in the British Isles.

rbg-web2.rbge.org.uk/bbs/bbs.htm

The British Bryological Society's guide to mosses and liverworts.

www.british-dragonflies.org.uk

The website of the British Dragonfly Society which encourages the conservation of dragonflies and their natural habitats.

www.wildflowerfinder.org.uk

Thousands of photographs and information about wildflowers set up by Roger Darlington.

www.orchidsofbritainandeurope.co.uk

Beautiful photographs of and information about European orchids.

www.bats.org.uk

The Bat Conservation Trust – an umbrella organization for the network of bat groups devoted to the conservation of bats and their habitats.

www.britishspiders.org.uk

The very wide-ranging website of the British Arachnological Society.

Index

Acknowledgements

I would like to thank everyone who has allowed me to work from their photographs, including Brian Sugden, Nigel Blake and particularly Barry Boswell. I'd also like to thank the following for their help and advice: The Natural History Museum, worms; Mike Sutcliffe, lichens; Howard Wallis, BBS Recorder for Surrey; Pam Taylor, dragonflies; John Peacock, orchids; and Pip Collyer, spiders.